HIDDEN HISTORY
of CIVIL WAR
FLORIDA

HIDDEN HISTORY
of CIVIL WAR
FLORIDA

ROBERT REDD

THE
History
PRESS

Published by The History Press
Charleston, SC
www.historypress.com

First published 2022

Manufactured in the United States

ISBN 9781467150873

Library of Congress Control Number: 2022933325

Notice: The information in this book is true and complete to the best of our knowledge. It is offered without guarantee on the part of the author or The History Press. The author and The History Press disclaim all liability in connection with the use of this book.

CONTENTS

Acknowledgements

A ny author will tell you that a single person does not write a book. Multiple people deserve recognition for their contributions. I have several people to thank. As always, my friend Jim Schmidt, who encouraged me in the writing of my first book. He has continued to be a support and is an excellent historian himself. Nick Wynne provided me with multiple pieces of research material for this book and has provided encouragement throughout my career. Nick is also lead administrator of the excellent Facebook group Florida's Civil War. I recommend joining. Michael C. Hardy has provided encouragement and guidance. If you are interested in the role of North Carolina in the Civil War, seek out Michael's books. Fellow Florida authors Jim Clark, Bob Grenier, Rob Mattson, Rick Kilby and others have always been supportive of my efforts and quick with a positive word. To those I have not singled out by name, please accept my apologies.

I would be remiss in not thanking Sarah Thorncroft at West Volusia Historical Society, Linda Hulvershorn at Southeast Volusia Historical Society and Fayn LeVeille and Heather Files at Halifax Historical Society for their support and assistance. Each has provided support, information and encouragement along the way. These women are prime examples of why you should support your local historical society.

To the folks at Arcadia Publishing, with a special shout-out to Joe Gartrell, I send my thanks. I would like to give a special thanks to copyeditor Zoe Ames, who has improved this manuscript 100 percent. This is my fifth book with Arcadia, and I hope to work with everybody again soon.

I have been working on this manuscript while attending classes at American Public University, working on my MA in public history. It has been neck and neck, as to which I would finish first—this book or my degree. My degree won out. To my professors and classmates, I thank you. You have pushed me, taught me, made me think and, if I have done my job properly, made me a better researcher and writer.

It has been a tough couple of years for my mother, having lost both her mother (my grandmother) and husband (my dad). She stays strong, however, and is always supportive. I appreciate it.

To my beautiful wife, Christina, thanks for your continued love and support. Your ability to accept piles of books and printed materials exceeds any realistic expectation I could have. How about we take Ruby to the dog park to celebrate finishing this book!

INTRODUCTION

Often, people view the state of Florida with a side-eye toward both its contribution to the Confederate effort during the Civil War and the perceived lack of scholarship on this limited role. During the war, a Northern newspaper referred to Florida as the "smallest tadpole in the dirty pool of secession."[1] For those who study the role of the Sunshine State in the war, both of these generalities could not be further from the truth.

First, let us address the obvious. There is little doubt that Florida was by far the smallest state in terms of population in the new Confederate States of America. The 1860 census shows the state having a total population of just over 140,000. Of this number, approximately 79,000 were free citizens and 61,000 were enslaved. Arkansas, the next smallest in population, had more than three times the total population of Florida, with approximately 435,000 residents: 324,000 free and 111,000 enslaved.

With a population as small as it was, Florida's workforce contribution was, of course, much smaller than those of all other states. While Arkansas supplied 74,000 Confederate troops, Florida sent 15,000 of its young men to fight in a war seldom waged within its borders.[2]

Florida Confederates fought in both the eastern and western theaters of the war. Known as the Florida Brigade in both theaters, Florida regiments served in the Army of Northern Virginia and the Army of Tennessee. Florida soldiers saw battle in crucial engagements such as Antietam, Gettysburg, Chickamauga, Atlanta and many others. Colonel David Lang and the Florida Brigade were with the Army of Northern Virginia when General Robert E. Lee surrendered his troops at Appomattox.

A fair question for residents of the state at the time might have been: What are you hoping to gain by fighting for the Confederacy? By March 1862, General Robert E. Lee was ordering troops withdrawn from the state and sent to the front lines elsewhere, leaving the state with few defenses and a long, inviting coastline for the Union to potentially exploit. Lee's orders to Brigadier General J.H. Trapier read, in part, "The Secretary, in his instructions, directed that the only troops to be retained in Florida were those employed in the defense of Apalachicola, and I wished you to understand that our necessities might limit us to the defense of that avenue through Florida into Georgia."[3]

The women and children remaining on the home front must have felt abandoned. The Confederate government sent their husbands, sons, brothers and uncles to far-off lands to fight an enemy that spoke the same language, looked similar to them and, just two years prior, could have been their friend. For the women left behind, the slaves needed tending, crops needed planting and harvesting and mouths needed to be fed. None of this was an easy proposition, and these tasks only became more difficult as the war dragged on.

Not only did Florida contribute troops to the Confederate cause, but Florida recruits loyal to the Union also fought against the Confederacy. Approximately two thousand men, both White and African American, fought against secession and the creation of a new government. As Tyler Campbell has written:

While many Whites throughout the Deep South embraced the ideology expressed by the secession commissioners, a large minority disagreed with secession and with the formation of the Confederate States of America that followed. Dissent took various forms and evolved as the war progressed, but all dissenters shared a desire to change the conditions thrust upon them because of secession. Some dissenters took up arms against the newly formed country and joined the Union Army.[4]

For African Americans, the goal was to secure their freedom from the bonds of slavery. Florida recruits joined regiments such as the Eighth and Thirty-Fifth United States Colored Troops, the Fifty-Fourth Massachusetts, and others. Black soldiers played considerable roles at the battles of Olustee and Natural Bridge, the two largest engagements in Florida. Confederates often singled out Black soldiers for extra attention and punishment during and after combat. At the Battle of Olustee, Colonel Abner McCormick of the Second Florida Cavalry told his troops, "Do not take any negro prisoners in this fight." Union participants reported seeing atrocities inflicted upon wounded Black soldiers.

Black troops did not serve in the army exclusively but were also a part of the Gulf Blockading Squadron. These former slaves played a crucial role in helping snuff out salt-making operations along the coasts. In the days prior to refrigeration, salt was crucial in preserving meat. Slaves had carried out much of the labor at saltworks. Now free, they often guided Union troops to the salt-making kettles and played a role in destroying them.

In spite of the positive role Black soldiers were playing, they were by no means treated as equals in the Union service. As historian Larry Eugene Rivers bluntly states, "Black soldiers and sailors faced unequal treatment when it came to wages, assignments, and overall treatment." This was not just a localized instance but was rather a formalized policy enacted by Secretary of the Navy Gideon Wells. Wells ruled that Black soldiers "be allowed…no higher rating than boys, at a compensation of $10 per month and one ration per day." Black soldiers usually earned less than 60 percent of equivalent White soldiers' pay.

Black residents who were not officially in Union service still often proved a valuable asset to the cause. In Jacksonville, Black residents used the Bethel Baptist Institutional Church as a de facto hospital, caring for wounded Union troops. Many Black residents served as cooks for Union regiments or provided other labor assistance. Despite having short rations themselves, many provided food, often from their owners' lands, to Union forces.[5]

For those new to Civil War studies, the state of Florida can be perplexing. It would seem there would be plenty to read; however, a trip to the bookstore would lead a student to feel otherwise. I would put forth that this is caused by the overall lack of fighting in the state. Every square inch of the Gettysburg battlefield has a microhistory written about it. Other campaigns and battles are now getting that type of treatment as well. For Florida, there are not such options. However, as nonmilitary aspects of the war are now being studied in more detail, I would expect to see additional study of Florida's key role in future.

There are a few basic works that many chain stores will carry, some of them by your friendly local Arcadia Publishing authors. Be sure to look for any titles by Nick Wynne. Dr. Wynne is both knowledgeable and engaging. If you are lucky, you may also find a few other standard titles that might be worthy of your time. Make sure to check the store's regional section rather than the two shelves of Civil War books.

What you are not going to find at a chain store, however, is the depth of work that is available. The historiography on Florida in the war is actually impressive, in comparison to what we have been led to believe. It just takes a bit of work to dig up the research of the past. Heck, the impressive level of academic work being released about Florida in the war today is not so easily found in the wild. It will take some digging, a special order at your local independent bookseller, a good library and access to PALMM and other academic databases.

The most obvious place to start is with bibliographies. When I first started studying history, the best advice I received from others was to mine the bibliographies of anything I was reading and then mine the bibliographies of those works. It is through this constant reviewing of literature that one can realize the study of Florida in the Civil War did not start in the last few decades.

A few of the primary texts on Florida in the war are outdated in terms of research and interpretation, unfortunately. *The Civil War and Reconstruction in Florida,* written by William Watson Davis, is a monster at more than seven hundred pages and is more than one hundred years old. Davis was a disciple of William Archibald Dunning, a professor at Columbia University and the namesake of the Dunning School. The Dunning School subscribed to a conservative outlook toward the efforts of Reconstruction. Radical Republican efforts were shunned and considered in error. The Dunning School played a significant role in early twentieth-century Southern writing, with students writing major works on the war in Alabama, Arkansas, Georgia, Mississippi, North Carolina, South Carolina and Texas. While there is historiographical value to this work, one should read it with a highly critical eye.[6]

A more modern but still sixty-year-old work is John E. Johns's *Florida During the Civil War.* At fewer than three hundred pages, the book is much more manageable than Davis's. Johns's book covers nonmilitary affairs, showing that Florida suffered hardships other than those of a military nature.

For those looking for a more modern interpretation, seek out the work of Tracy J. Revels. Revels's book *Florida's Civil War: Terrible Sacrifices* is a good starting point. At fewer than two hundred pages and under thirty dollars, this academically vetted work covers the major subjects related to the war and is recommended for those just coming to the subject. While not without critics, this title should be on the shelves of any student of the Civil War in Florida.[7]

For readers interested in the meat of the war, the fighting, Olustee is the major subject in Florida history. After much consideration, I made the decision not to discuss the battle in this book, my reasoning being that there are several full-length books on the subject that readers are better off finding. William H. Nulty's *Confederate Florida: The Road to Olustee* is the best book-length treatment and is occasionally available on chain store shelves. I also recommend Daniel Shafer's *Thunder on the River: The Civil War in Northeast Florida.* While covering more ground than just Olustee, this is a well-researched and well-written volume that should be on the shelf of every student of Florida history.

If you are interested in learning more about the actions of Florida troops during the war, there are two excellent brigade histories available. For those interested in the eastern war, I suggest seeking out *A Small but Spartan Band: The Florida Brigade in Lee's Army of Northern Virginia* by Zack C. Waters and James C. Edmonds. If the war in the west is your preference, Jonathan C. Sheppard has written the excellent *By the Noble Daring of Her Sons: The Florida Brigade of the Army of Tennessee.* Both should be standard references for years to come.

Despite Florida's being a small state, slavery was an issue as war broke out. The diverse regions of Florida led to differences, as north and middle Florida were more plantation-based and east and west Florida relied more on small farms with fewer slaves. Slavery is a large and complex subject, and therefore, I have not included it here. Rather, I recommend that you seek out a copy of *Slavery in Florida: Territorial Days to Emancipation*, written by Larry Eugene Rivers. Dr. Rivers's book is readily available and has received generous praise. As a review in the *American Historical Review* states, "[Rivers] makes sound judgments and analyses based upon copious research....The book's readability will make it accessible to general readers as well as scholars and will ensure that it reaches a wide audience."[8]

Several key figures of the war are from, or have ties to, Florida. Biographies on these men are a bit spotty overall. Perhaps the best-known Confederate general to come from Florida is Edmund Kirby Smith. The most commonly cited biography on Smith is *General Edmund Kirby Smith, C.S.A.*, written by Joseph H. Parks and published by Louisiana State University Press in 1962. In 1992, the publisher released a paperback reprint. William Wing Loring, who also fought in the Egyptian army, is the subject of the biography *W.W. Loring: Florida's Forgotten General*, written by James W. Raab. Raab has also penned *J. Patton Anderson, Confederate General: A Biography.* As Michael C. Hardy has shown, biographies on Florida Civil War generals are much needed in the literature.[9]

One of the most amazing stories of a Civil War manuscript has to be that of Dr. Esther Hill Hawks. In 1975, three bound composition books of Hawks's writings were found discarded during an apartment renovation occurring in Essex County, Massachusetts. These diaries begin in October 1862 and end in November 1866. The diaries' editor, Gerald Schwartz, believes it likely there was originally a fourth volume that covered Hawks's time in Florida. Those who have read Sarah Morgan, Mary Chestnut and others would be wise to seek out the writings of Esther Hill Hawks. Hawks's papers reside in the Library of Congress, while the three diaries are still in private hands.[10]

If you are interested in photography, there are several good resources available. Your local bookstore might have a copy of Bob Grenier's *Central Florida's Civil War Veterans.* Bob has scoured archives and collections looking for examples of people, places and events associated with the war. Accompanying each image is an informative caption. It is worth finding a copy. Bob is also an engaging speaker. If you get a chance to see one of his presentations, I recommend attending. Also, be sure to check the Library of Congress and Florida Memory websites. These amazing archives can keep a researcher busy for hours. Just type in your search term and be amazed at what is available. The Library of Congress often has high-resolution scans available for free download. You may download low-resolution images at Florida Memory, and high-quality scans or prints are available at very reasonable prices. Maybe you will find that distant relative you have been seeking.

I previously mentioned the need for a good library in your studies. This can certainly be an academic library, but that is not required. Many public libraries have surprisingly strong collections, excellent noncirculating collections and reference librarians who are more than eager to assist. Interlibrary loan is your friend.

Students will find much of the best published research on Civil War Florida in the *Florida Historical Quarterly.* Some Florida libraries subscribe to this excellent journal, and many others have back issue collections available. Be sure to check with your local historical society, as well. If you prefer to search and read from the comfort of your home, you may use the PALMM (Publication of Archival Library & Museum Materials) online database service to access all but the most recent FHQ articles. Be sure to look at JSTOR for academic journal articles, as well.

Chapter 1

SECESSION

When Frances Kirby Smith, mother of future Confederate general and commander of the Trans-Mississippi Department of the Confederate army Edmund Kirby Smith, stated in early 1860, "Southern men and Southern women will not sit down with folded hands if the masses elect a Black Republican president," it was unlikely she had any premonition as to how true her words would be.[11]

Once the conservative Democratic Party nominated James Buchanan for president in 1856, John C. Breckenridge became an ideal running mate. He had national name recognition and could appeal to both Northern and Southern voters in the party. The Democratic Party ran on a platform of states' rights, the Kansas-Nebraska Act and the annexation of proslavery Cuba. When the November election was held, the Buchanan/Breckenridge ticket handily defeated the Know-Nothing Party candidates Millard Fillmore and Andrew Jackson Donelson in both the popular and electoral college votes. In Florida, Buchanan and Breckenridge polled over 56 percent of the vote and received the states' three electoral college votes.

John C. Breckenridge was a former two-term congressional representative from Kentucky who had played a key role in formulating the Kansas-Nebraska Act of 1854. His view that popular sovereignty would help determine the outcome of the slavery debate proved misguided and helped lead to the clashes that became known as "Bleeding Kansas."

This proven conservative record of accomplishment led to a Breckenridge presidential nomination in 1860. However, the issue of slavery fractured

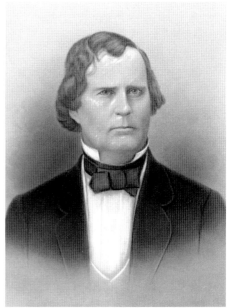

Left: John C. Breckenridge served as vice president under James Buchanan. He was later to run unsuccessfully for president in 1860 as the "Southern Democrat" against rivals Abraham Lincoln, Stephen A. Douglas and John Bell. Breckenridge was the leading vote-getter in Florida, with slightly over eight thousand ballots. *Library of Congress.*

Right: Madison Starke Perry served as Florida governor from 1857 through 1861. It was under Perry's leadership that Florida seceded from the Union. During the Civil War, Perry was commissioned as colonel of the Seventh Florida Infantry, a position he held until resigning over health issues. *State Archives of Florida.*

the Democratic party. Northern Democrats, led by Stephen A. Douglas, believed that decisions regarding slavery issued by the Supreme Court were legally binding and were to be adhered to. Southern Democrats broke from this view, held a separate convention in Baltimore, Maryland, during June and adopted a platform including a proslavery stance.[12]

As the election of 1860 drew near, the Florida press flexed its muscles in support of Southern Democrats. The *Cedar Key Telegraph* condemned those supporting Douglas or John Bell, editorializing, "The Douglas-Bell men of the South, like Wendell Phillips, have gone crazy—they have entered into a covenant with death and a league with hell, and are doing all within their power to elect Mr. Lincoln."[13]

The results of the presidential election in November 1860 in Florida were predictable and provided Southern Democrat candidate John C.

Breckenridge with slightly over eight thousand votes, or more than 62 percent of the state's ballots. John Bell, the Constitutional Union candidate, and Stephen A. Douglas lagged considerably behind, not even equaling Breckinridge's votes between them. Noticeably absent was the "Black Republican," Abraham Lincoln, who did not appear on the ballot.[14]

The national election of 1860 was a contentious one. Many historians consider the split in the Democratic Party to be a significant factor in the election of Abraham Lincoln. Perhaps, but the reality is that the two factions were never going to work together and present a united party. Sectional lines had been clearly drawn within the party, and coming together to defeat the Republican Lincoln was not possible. Despite not appearing on the ballot in ten states, Lincoln still garnered just under 40 percent of the national popular vote and 180 electoral college votes. Douglas and Breckenridge combined did not equal Lincoln's total in the popular vote, and they only earned 84 combined electoral college votes.

Events of the 1850s coupled with the national election of Abraham Lincoln caused a boiling over with many elected officials in Florida. With events such as the Kansas-Nebraska Act and John Brown's raid fresh in their minds, the election of Abraham Lincoln became the tipping point. The press often clamored for action by their elected officials. A November 3, 1860 editorial in the *St. Augustine Examiner* boldly stated, in the event of a possible Lincoln victory, "What shall Florida do? Secede of course."[15] In fact, many Southerners were under the misguided opinion "that the South was so important to the economic interests of the western states and to Great Britain and France that they would use force to hold off any government attempt to prevent secession."[16]

On November 27, 1860, Governor Madison Starke Perry delivered a stinging message to the state legislature, exclaiming, "The only hope Southern states have for domestic peace…or for future respectability and prosperity, is dependent on their action now; and that the proper actions is—Secession from our faithless, perjured confederates."[17] Only three days later, on November 30, Governor Perry signed a bill calling for a December 22 election date to select delegates for a January 3, 1861 convention to be held in Tallahassee.[18]

Campaigning was straightforward. The ultimate decision had already been determined: secession. It became a matter of how the state should move ahead. The primary options were to secede immediately, less than sixteen years after having been granted admission to the Union, or to work in cooperation with other states and perhaps make a more significant impact.

The fire-breathing immediate secessionists, including then Governor Perry and Governor-elect John Milton, ruled the election, taking about 60 percent of the seats. These men would help shape the direction of Florida, and ultimately the Union, for the next four years.[19]

On Thursday, January 3, 1861, delegates arrived for the Florida Convention in Tallahassee to determine the path Florida would follow in light of the recent election of Abraham Lincoln. Historian Ralph A. Wooster has compiled an interesting look at these White men to determine how they were alike and what differences they may have had.

Wooster determined the average age of a delegate was 42.5 years, placing them solidly in middle age. Their geographic origins showed a wide diversity, with sixteen states, the Bahamas and Ireland represented. Only seven delegates were native Floridians. Attendees had been born in several Yankee states, including Maine, Connecticut, Massachusetts, Vermont, Indiana, Pennsylvania and Maryland.

As might be expected with the rural landscape of the state, twenty-five members were classified as farmers in the 1860 census. An additional ten were enumerated as merchants.

Determining the wealth of the average delegate proves much more difficult. Wooster proposes that the average delegate's wealth was probably somewhere around $25,000, divided between real and personal property. There were extreme differences in wealth, with E.E. Simpson of Santa Rosa County showing a total wealth of over $2,500,000, while nearly half of the delegates claimed less than $5,000 in real property on the 1860 census.

At the forefront of the secessionist movement was the issue of slavery. Slave ownership among the elected delegates is an important issue to understand. Of the sixty-nine delegates, Wooster has identified fifty-one, or an overwhelming 74 percent, as being slaveholders. The average holdings for delegates owning slaves was 35.6 slaves, while the average for all convention delegates was lower: 26.7. Twenty-six members held more than 20 slaves, while eleven members owned more than 50 persons. The largest slave owners were G.W. Parkhill, with 172, and George T. Ward, who owned 170 slaves. Both men hailed from Leon County, home of Tallahassee, the state capital.[20]

Tallahassee was a hive of activity in early January 1861 as the Secession Convention came to order on the third. Politicians, onlookers and out-of-state lobbyists, such as the exceedingly vocal secessionist Edmund Ruffin, filled local hotels to overflowing. After a short assembly, the convention adjourned until January 5, a strategic move on two fronts: President James

COLONEL GEORGE T. WARD.

JOHN C. McGEHEE,
President of the Florida
Secession Convention

Left: Colonel George T. Ward was a large slaveholder who served during the Florida Secession Convention; he was the last to sign the articles of secession. Ward was later elected to the Confederate congress and served as a colonel in the Second Florida Infantry. *State Archives of Florida.*

Right: John C. McGehee served as the president of the Florida Secession Convention. McGehee, a native of South Carolina who had migrated to Madison County, Florida, was an immediate secessionist who guided the convention with a firm hand toward leaving the Union. *State Archives of Florida.*

Buchanan had called for a day of fasting and prayer to address the heated political situation, and adjourning also allowed extra travel time for delegates who resided in the southernmost sections of the state.[21]

When the convention reconvened on January 5, delegates elected John C. McGehee, a large slaveholder from Madison County, as president. McGehee was a native of South Carolina and was an ardent immediate secessionist. His secessionist views were well known, and he had been a leader in the Florida Southern Rights Movement of the 1850s.

Members of the convention came in two stripes, the radical immediate secessionists and the conservative cooperationists, with each putting forth a secession plan. George Parkhill put forth the conservative plan, which was really a delaying tactic. The cooperationists were not interested in cooperating with the federal government but rather wanted to wait until the border states of Georgia and Alabama had committed to secession. At that time, the issue would be decided through a vote of eligible citizens.

Former federal judge McQueen McIntosh, who had resigned his position upon the election of Abraham Lincoln, presented the radical plan. It stated that the convention had the duty to declare secession a protected constitutional right and that the convention could act on behalf of the state populace they had been elected to represent. Conventioneers tabled both plans until Monday, January 7.[22]

When they reconvened on January 7, those attending the convention were prodded to action upon hearing speeches from the immediate secessionists Edward C. Bullock of Alabama, Leonidas W. Spratt of South Carolina and noted firebrand Edmund Ruffin.[23]

Edmund Ruffin recalled the events of the morning. Mr. Bullock of Alabama spoke first, for approximately forty-five minutes. He spoke in favor of immediate secession and the formation of a union of Southern states. Mr. Spratt followed, reading the South Carolina secession ordinance and recounting the address "On Relations of the Slave-Holding States of North America" before concluding with his own comments on actions in South Carolina.

In what might be considered a staged moment, John C. Pelot of Alachua County made a motion that Mr. Ruffin be allowed to address the convention. This motion was approved, and Mr. Ruffin, claiming not to speak for Virginia, addressed the delegates. Ruffin encouraged early action by Florida and its adjoining states. These actions and the show of solidarity would help lead border states, such as Virginia, to secession. Ruffin wrote later, "I spoke earnestly, and but for a short time and seemed to have pleased my auditors."[24]

Upon completion of comments from guests, the delegates returned to the work at hand. It was important to determine the path that the convention would follow. It was certainly obvious to those in attendance what the outcome was to be. The motion presented by the Honorable Mr. McIntosh was at the forefront. The cooperationist wing of the convention again attempted delaying tactics. They tried to add amendments to the resolution, again calling for a popular vote. This motion was voted down in what was a rather close vote, 43–24. When the McIntosh motion alone was presented for a vote, it was overwhelmingly approved, 62–5.[25]

With a path chosen, convention president McGehee appointed a committee of thirteen members, consisting of eight radicals and five conservatives, to begin preparing the Florida Ordinance of Secession.[26]

 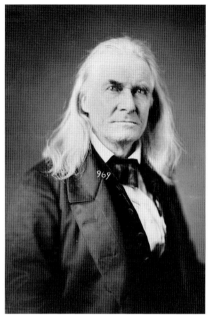

Left: Colonel Edward Bullock was an immediate secessionist from Alabama who addressed the Florida Secession Convention on January 7, 1861, and called for the creation of a union of Southern states. *Alabama Department of Archives and History.*

Right: Edmund Ruffin was a proponent of slavery who spoke at the Florida Secession Convention. He urged the state to act early, not to wait for those adjoining it. After the surrender of the Confederacy, Ruffin committed suicide rather than live under "Yankee rule." *Library of Congress.*

On January 9, the select committee presented their draft report and secession ordinance to the full delegation. While the five cooperationist committee members did not sign the report, neither did they produce documents of their own for consideration. Based on this lack of action, the convention only considered the single draft ordinance. After discussion, the ordinance as presented was deemed too vague, and the job of drafting a revised ordinance was given to the judiciary committee with instructions to report back in only one hour. This they did, producing the following draft:

> *We the people of the State of Florida in Convention assembled, do solemnly ordain, publish, and declare,*
> *That the State of Florida hereby withdraws herself from the Confederacy of States existing under the name of the United States of America, and from the existing Government of the said States; and that all political*

connection between her and the Government of the said States ought to be, and the same is hereby totally annulled, and said Union of States dissolved; and the State of Florida is hereby declared a Sovereign and Independent Nation; and that all ordinances heretofore adopted, in so far as they create or recognize said Union, are rescinded; and all laws or parts of laws in force in this State, in so far as they recognized or assented to said Union, be and they are hereby repealed.[27]

Still grasping to reign in the radical element of the convention, cooperationists again attempted delaying tactics. Abraham K. Allison of Gadsden County proposed keeping the ordinance from going into effect until both Alabama and Georgia had seceded, or if either state did not secede, until the voters of the state had approved the ordinance. This amendment was voted down 42–27. George T. Ward then proposed delaying until after Alabama and Georgia seceded but did not require voter approval. Once the two neighbor states seceded, Florida would automatically secede. This proposal failed when put to a vote but with a closer tally, 39–30. Secessionists voted down three other delaying attempts before the cooperationists realized the futility of their efforts.[28]

After a week of work, the convention had reached its goal. On January 10, the delegates reconvened for a vote on the final ordinance language. Despite cooperationist objections to the outcome, all sixty-nine delegates attended. The tally was 62–7 in favor of ratification. At 12:22 p.m., the Florida Ordinance of Secession was declared adopted. Upon announcement, a tremendous roar of approval could be heard throughout the building.[29] While news traveled slowly in 1861, the secession celebrations were no less joyous days after the signing than if they had occurred on January 10. Towns and cities throughout the state celebrated the news.

Floridians did not all agree that secession was a positive. When cooperationist delegate George T. Ward stepped forward to sign the document, he declared, "When I die I want it inscribed upon my tombstone that I was the last man to give up the ship."[30] Ward was later elected to the Confederate Congress before being elected as colonel to the Second Florida Infantry Regiment. Colonel Ward was killed during the Battle of Williamsburg on May 5, 1862. His remains were interred at Bruton Parish Episcopal Church Cemetery in Williamsburg, Virginia.

Perhaps most vocal in his opposition was former Florida governor Richard Keith Call. Governor Call was a former Whig and known Unionist. Upon meeting a group of joyous secessionists bragging about what had been

Richard Keith Call served two separate terms as Florida territorial governor. Despite being the owner of approximately two hundred slaves, Call was a devoted Unionist who believed secession was in error. He was to be proven correct as the war played out. *State Archives of Florida.*

accomplished, Call replied, "And what have you done? You have opened the gates of Hell, from which shall flow the curses of the damned to sink you to perdition."[31]

Scholars have since debated whether or not the secession convention, in moving rapidly with the immediate secession plan, was acting upon the interests and values of Florida residents. Historian John F. Reiger has addressed this question in regards to the radicals. When they refused to allow a popular vote on the subject, "was this because they were simply in a hurry to make Florida the next state on the Confederate banner or was it rather because they were afraid that a popular vote would reveal a strong pro-Union undercurrent in a sea of secession"? Dorothy Dodd has questioned whether the rapid movement was due to a need for haste or a fear that a vote on secession could go down in defeat. It did not matter whether the White male voters would have voted for secession. Their surrogates did. Moreover, with that vote made on January 10, 1861, Florida was set on a path that would forever affect the state.[32]

Chapter 2

NOT A SHOT WAS FIRED

E quality in the Union and Nothing Less." So read the motto of the St. Augustine newspaper, the *Examiner*. Newspaper publisher Matthias Andreu and most locals were pro-secession and, for the time, not afraid to share these views. In discussing abolitionists, Andreu had gone so far as to say about them, "The day is possibly not distant, when such talk will be punished as treason, and it is not improbable, some one of them may adorn a gallows."[33]

It was not long before the *Examiner* was publishing the much-anticipated news coming out of Tallahassee. The January 19, 1861 edition brought excitement to the small coastal town with the news:

> *It is done. On Saturday afternoon several of our citizens who arrived from Tallahassee where the State convention had assembled and is not in session, brought us the intelligence that the Secession Ordinance had been passed by that body, declaring that Florida withdraws herself from the Confederacy of states existing under the name of the United States of America.*

With the rise in Confederate patriotism came a new flagpole that was erected in the downtown plaza. Under the direction of Mrs. Cooper Gibbs, local women sewed a new flag to fly over the town. Bishop Augustin Verot, the proslavery leader of the local Catholic church, believed that a religious revival was occurring. Local men were joining militia units, unaware that shortly they were to be sent to faraway places, fighting a war that would ultimately drain not just resources but also the spirit of many locals.

On January 5, 1861, Florida governor Madison Starke Perry ordered the seizure of "arsenal, arms, ammunition, stores, buildings, and other property now in possession of the General Government, and retain the same subject to my orders" in multiple state locations.[34] On January 7, this occurred at Fort Marion, in rather anticlimactic fashion. Fort Marion, more commonly known today as the Castillo de San Marcos, is the large coquina fort guarding the Matanzas River in St. Augustine. Ordnance Sergeant Henry Douglas reported the events of the day in a letter penned to Colonel H.K. Craig:

> *I am obliged to perform what is to me a painful duty, viz, to report to the Chief of Ordnance that all the military stores at this place were seized this morning by the order of the governor of the State of Florida. A company of volunteer soldiers marched to the barracks and took possession of me, and demanded peaceable possession of the keys to the fort and magazine. I demanded them to show me their authority. An aide-de-camp of the governor showed me his letter of instruction authorizing him to seize the property, and directing him to use what force might be necessary.*
>
> *Upon reflection I decided that the only alternative for me was to deliver the keys, under protest, and demand a receipt for the property. One thing certain, with the exception of the guns composing the armament of the water battery, the property seized is of no great value. The gentleman acting under the governor's instructions has promised to receipt to me for the stores.*[35]

With this action, the Confederacy had, without bloodshed, struck a blow in the state. Many of the militiamen did not stay long, however. They removed several of the large guns from the fort and took them north to Fort Clinch.

While the insurrectionists had struck an early blow, it was an unsure one at best. As occurred in many areas of the Confederacy, there was also Union support that could rise and undermine the proslavery efforts. Secession supporters raised what they called "vigilance committees." These committees kept open eyes and ears for slave agitators or those speaking against secession. Local Unionists such as Clarissa Anderson decided it best to protest silently in manners such as unsubscribing from the local newspaper. Frances Kirby Smith had previously described them: "These abolition scamps do not hesitate to enjoy our fine climate & hospitalities (when they can get them) hating us inwardly, and outwardly doing all they dare."[36]

Not a shot was fired as the city of St. Augustine changed hands twice during the Civil War. This photo at Fort Marion, taken by photographer Samuel A. Cooley, shows Union soldiers and their tents along the terreplein level. *Library of Congress.*

As the resolve of Abraham Lincoln hardened, things became more difficult in the old city. Real concern washed over the town with the stated Union goal of retaking any federal property seized by Confederates. Would the Union Navy storm up the Matanzas River and retake Fort Marion? If so, when?

The Union blockade and lack of men at home to provide labor created serious shortages in St. Augustine. Despite their ability to grow and raise some types of food, residents depended upon outside sources to complete their diet. An archaeological dig in the 1980s showed that Civil War–era residents often lived on a subsistence diet similar to residents of the town three hundred years prior.[37]

Blockade running was a profitable, yet dangerous, career choice. Blockade runners' long, shallow drafted ships typically ran in the dark of night to try to avoid detection by Union naval troops. The Confederate government had ordered lighthouses to extinguish their lights, causing additional danger to ship captains. In St. Augustine, locals led by Paul Arnau extinguished the light by removing the vital lens pieces. Arnau and his men did not stop in St. Augustine. They traveled south, extinguishing lights at Cape Canaveral, Jupiter Inlet and Key Biscayne before Arnau proudly reported his actions to Governor Perry. Later in 1861 and into 1862, Arnau was to serve as mayor of St. Augustine.[38]

Further making life difficult for locals now under Confederate rule was the decline in the tourist trade. Even in the 1860s, residents and out-of-towners considered St. Augustine a tourist destination, and the winter 1861–62 season was a difficult one for merchants. In attempting to refocus tourism efforts, the local paper suggested marketing the town as a summer destination for Southerners rather than focusing on efforts to bring cold Northerners south.

A letter written in 1861 sums up the difficult situation being felt locally:

> These "secession" movements have made quite a revolution in & about this "ancient City." Once it was the resort of many invalids & strangers, but is now wholly deserted by them. Those who reside here are in very straightened circumstances & live "from hand to mouth." Provisions are very scarce and dear & those who are not too poor to move seem determined to leave. Without giving further details I can only say that "St. Augustine" is far from a desirable place to live in.[39]

Confederate troops abandoned the city when, in early 1862, officers ordered the majority of men north to fight in what they considered territory that was more valuable. In leaving the small coastal town defenseless, Robert E. Lee stated, "The small force posted at Saint Augustine serves only as an invitation to attack."[40]

It was not long before the Union Navy took action on newly abandoned cities. On February 28, 1862, a fleet of twenty-six ships left Hilton Head, South Carolina, with the stated goal of occupying coastal towns. On March 8, the steamer *Keystone State* and others arrived off the coast of St. Augustine. On March 11, Commander C.R.P. Rogers and sailors from the USS *Wabash* rowed ashore under a flag of truce and were met by a similar flag flying at Fort Marion. Mayor Christobal Bravo met the Union men at the wharf. Bravo had only recently taken over as mayor after the resignation of loyal Confederate Paul Arnau.

Mayor Bravo greeted the sailors and officers, welcoming them to the Government House building, where the city council had convened in order to hear out the surrender demands. Having encountered no opposition and sensing none was forthcoming, Commander Rogers's demands were rather simple. Bravo and the current council were allowed to continue governing the city as long as they accepted the authority of the United States. Not having much in the way of options, Bravo and the council quickly agreed. As a symbol of Union control of the town, Commander Rogers requested that a Union flag be flown over Fort Marion.

Union occupation of the town was not met with universal support. The flagpole, only recently raised in the plaza, was unceremoniously chopped down in order to prevent a Union flag from flying on it. Frances Kirby Smith, never one to hold back her tongue or pen, wrote of town leadership, "Old Bravo" and the council "much like him, all low ignorant Minorcans, puffed up by their devotion to office, had raised the white flag as soon as two row boats rounded the point—and afterwards assisted in raising on the Fort their flag."[41]

In reporting his success to Flag Officer Samuel F. Du Pont, Rogers wrote, in part:

> *About 1,500 persons remain in St. Augustine, about one-fifth of the inhabitants having fled.*
>
> *I believe that there are many citizens who are earnestly attached to the Union, a large number who are silently opposed to it, and a still larger number who care very little about the matter. I think that nearly all the men acquiesce in the condition of affairs we are now establishing.*
>
> *There is much violent and pestilent feeling among the women. They seem to mistake treason for courage, and have a theatrical desire to figure as heroines.*
>
> *Their minds have doubtless been filled with the falsehoods so industriously circulated in regard to the lust and hatred of our troops.*
>
> *On the night before our arrival a party of women assembled in front of the barracks and cut down the flagstaff, in order that it might not be used to support the old flag.*
>
> *The men seem anxious to conciliate us in every way.*
>
> *There is a great scarcity of provisions in the place. There seems to be no money except the wretched paper currency of the rebellion, and much poverty exists.*[42]

With these words, the second bloodless seizing of Fort Marion was concluded. St. Augustine was to remain unchallenged in Union hands for the remainder of the war.

Chapter 3

THE TROOPS MUST BE FED

An army marches on its stomach" is an old phrase often attributed to Napoleon Bonaparte. Whether the French political and military leader ever uttered these words is irrelevant. The truth of the saying is evident. A hungry army cannot fight at the optimum level. Keeping an army well fed is a primary role of officers. Field officers during the Civil War relied heavily on commissary departments to keep their men fed. When these departments failed, as often occurred, armies were left to fend for themselves, often in unfamiliar territory.

From the start of the war, Florida ranchers were supplying beef to Confederate troops. At first, however, this beef was used to feed troops stationed in the state. Much of the supply was sent to the Cedar Key area, a location heavily fortified in anticipation of a Union attack. Inflationary pressures, which would seriously harm the Confederacy, were already showing as beef prices escalated from six cents per pound to more than eight cents per pound in early 1862.[43]

At the outbreak of the war, the Confederate government purchased cattle from many areas—and not just Florida. They would face several obstacles in obtaining cattle, including the invading Union forces. While cattle were a sustainable resource, they had to be managed properly. Cattle ranchers understood this, but oftentimes field officers and leaders in Richmond did not. Cattle butchering could not occur at will. Stock had to be retained for breeding and replenishment. Cattle good enough for providing meat for troops took years to raise. Cattle being raised for market took considerable grain to reach optimal size. Cattle ranchers then marched the herds to a transport location, putting stress upon the animal and lowering the quality of the beef. Time and grain were things the Confederacy was lacking.[44]

By early 1862, through the final surrenders, Confederate armies were showing the effects of decreased rations. Generals such as Braxton Bragg, P.G.T. Beauregard and Joseph E. Johnston leaned heavily on Florida to deliver much-needed cattle to the troops. While the state did provide at least seventy-five thousand head in support of the war effort, these numbers paled in comparison to what generals believed was available.[45]

During the early phases of the war, the Confederate government hired civilian agents in an attempt to help locate and deliver cattle northward. Confederate guidelines stated that these agents were to work directly with ranchers. The Confederate government believed that, in this way, cattle speculators would be put out of business and inflationary pressures lowered. Florida cattleman Jacob Summerlin was hired to be the civilian agent for the state of Florida.

Jacob "Jake" Summerlin had developed a reputation that perhaps made him most suited for this role of civilian agent. Summerlin claimed to have been the first White person born in the state after it became an American territory. Historians have questioned his birth date, however. Summerlin is buried in Bartow, Florida, and his headstone states his birth date was February 22, 1820. Other sources place it between 1819 and 1825. The exact date, and Summerlin's claim, are not relevant to his story, however.[46]

Those who knew him considered Summerlin be an astute businessperson. A legend states that in 1848, when Jake's father passed away, the younger Summerlin inherited several slaves that he sold or traded for cattle. Whether this is true or not is debatable. We are on firmer ground in understanding that around this time Summerlin did purchase fifty head of cattle from James Whitten of Georgia. These would help build the foundation of Summerlin's herd.[47]

In 1849, Summerlin received appointment as postmaster for the small settlement of Hitchepucksassa, an area that was settled during the Second Seminole War. According to Summerlin biographers Joe A. Akerman and J. Mark Akerman, the name Hitchepucksassa has several possible meanings, including "tobacco fields," "many pipes" or "the place where the moon plants the colors of the rainbow, and the sun draws them out in the flowers."[48] No matter the translation, the small area was a popular trading post, providing settlers with goods such as saddles, blankets, guns, clothes, seed and more.

Jacob "Jake" Summerlin was one of the leading cattle ranchers in Florida prior to the Civil War. During the war, the Commissary Department appointed him commissary sergeant, with a directive to provide twenty-five thousand head of cattle per year to the Confederate army. After his term, he took up blockade running and smuggling to supplement his lost income. *State Archives of Florida.*

By the early 1850s, Summerlin was paying taxes on more than 1,200 head of cattle located in Orange County. By 1854, Summerlin was becoming quite wealthy. He owned more than 2,000 head of cattle spread throughout Orange and Hillsborough Counties. He also owned more than three hundred acres of land.[49]

The census of 1860 shows the Summerlin family, misspelled Sumerlin, living in Hillsborough County. Jacob is listed as a farmer and butcher with real estate valued at $4,500 and a personal estate of $48,000. The slave census of the same year shows Summerlin owning a total of five slaves, four males and a single female.[50]

It was during the last years of the 1850s and through 1860 that Summerlin and others earned considerable revenue selling cattle to the Cuban and West Indies markets. Summerlin began doing business with James McKay, a cattle shipper out of Tampa. In addition to Summerlin's own livestock, Summerlin and McKay purchased cattle at around five dollars per head, selling them for around fifteen dollars on the Cuban market. When drought killed off more than two thousand head of cattle in 1860, the partners relocated their shipping operation to the mouth of the Peace River, near modern-day Punta Gorda. Here, they continued operations, shipping thousands of head of cattle, aware that, soon, either Union or Confederate troops would shutter their operation.[51]

When it came time to choose sides after secession, Summerlin chose the Confederacy. This was not out of any overriding belief in the cause, as we have seen he was not a large slaveholder, rather, he saw his allegiance as being to his state. His business interests were in Florida and Florida was Confederate. So would be Jacob Summerlin.[52]

The Union blockade of 1861 severely hindered but did not stop Summerlin and McKay from shipping cattle. Their operation was only now on a much smaller scale, with higher stakes. McKay was still making small trips to Cuba, leaving under cover of darkness, using his familiarity with the area to slip past any waiting Union ships.[53]

In 1861, the Confederate army was purchasing cattle, but these animals mainly fed soldiers stationed inside Florida. Some cattle, however, did make their way north to feed Confederate troops in the field. The Confederate government was already beginning to see Florida as a savior should food supply lines be cut off. General John K. Jackson, writing later in the war to other field leaders, stated:

> *From Official and other data I learn that the product of army supplies will amount annually to 25,000 head of beeves, equal to 10,000,000 pound; 1,000 hogsheads of sugar; 100,000 gallons of syrup, equal by exchange to 4,000,000 pounds of bacon; 50,000 sides of leather; 100,000 barrels of fish (if labor afforded), equal to 20,000,000 pounds of fish. Oranges, lemons, arrowroot, salt, blockade goods, iron, etc. Counting the bacon at one-third pound and beef and fish at one pound to the ration there are of meat rations 45,000,000—enough to supply 250,000 for six months.*[54]

Jackson was clearly misled, delusional or outright lying. Florida had neither the resources nor the labor to supply this level of goods, especially when most able-bodied men were in military service and residents on the home front were facing hard times.

With his large herds and influence in the cattle industry, Jacob Summerlin received a commission as commissary sergeant in the Commissary Department of the Confederate government in the fall of 1861. Confederate commissary general Lucius B. Northrop believed these new commissary sergeants would ensure that every state was providing needed resources to the troops in the field, no matter the location.[55]

Summerlin's commission was a two-year term, and he was contracted to deliver 25,000 head per year, a goal he hoped to achieve through his own herds and cattle purchased from other ranchers. Prices were to range from eight dollars to ten dollars per head. These prices should have made Summerlin a considerable profit. Unfortunately, that did not turn out to be the case. In his first year, Summerlin received payment in Confederate cash. Not having full faith in the value of Confederate paper, Summerlin traveled to Charleston, where he exchanged the script for bonds that were redeemable in gold—gold he was never to receive. Despite his growing unease, Summerlin continued with the second year of his commission.[56]

The year 1862 would prove difficult for Summerlin. Confederate troops in the western theater of the war were beginning to experience meat shortages. Beef supplies from Texas were not arriving regularly, and Braxton Bragg had less than two months of salted meat available for his command. The Union presence in northeast Florida, particularly St. Augustine and Jacksonville, made acquiring cattle from this region extremely difficult. Union raiders, both on land and on the St. Johns River, confiscated cattle, destroyed property and freed slaves that they encountered.[57]

At the end of his appointment, Summerlin left the employ of the Confederate government. He and his former partner James McKay took up smuggling and blockade running, basing their operations out of Punta Rassa. Summerlin and McKay made at least six successful blockade runs, selling cattle and returning with needed goods such as flour, sugar and salt.[58]

By 1863, the state of Florida found itself becoming a leading source of beef for several Confederate armies, including the Army of the Tennessee, and for troops defending Charleston. Several factors led to this increased need for Florida beef, the primary being Confederate losses in Tennessee during the 1862–63 struggles. Military losses in Tennessee and Kentucky proved exceedingly difficult to overcome. Prior to the troops retreating, General Bragg's men had been able to live off the fertile Tennessee land that supplied an abundance of both beef and pork. Secondly, in July 1863, the fall of Vicksburg and the loss of control of the Mississippi River led to a slowdown or complete halt in beef supplies from the Trans-Mississippi region. It was vital for the Confederate Commissary Bureau to find dependable sources of meat for the troops.[59]

In an attempt to ease the collection and purchase of cattle, hold down inflationary price spirals and reduce smuggling efforts, Confederate commissary general Lucius B. Northrop created a policy calling for commissary agents in each state. The commissary agent would be responsible for controlling collection and shipment of all food supplies within his state. He would work with both the Confederate Commissary Department and the soldiers in charge of supplies for armies operating in, or near, his state. Northrup provided guidance allowing these state officers the authority to subdivide their states into districts, with the goal of raising efficiency.

Northrup's goal was to create a network so that no matter where an army was located, there would be supplies available for its use.[60] Northrup appears to have forgotten that Confederate troops were rapidly losing navigable river access. Railroad mileage, already at a disadvantage at the beginning of the war, was being destroyed at every opportunity by Union forces. As Northrup and others were to find out in the following years, this lack of transportation was just one of a myriad of problems facing them. Difficulty in finding and purchasing cattle, finding cattle in good enough condition to walk the necessary distances to available transport facilities, Union interference and competition, unwilling sellers and other issues plagued the Confederate efforts, all to the detriment of the soldiers in the field.

It was on June 26, 1863, that Pleasant W. White was named chief commissary for the state of Florida, receiving the rank of major in the Confederate army. White accepted this role less than two weeks prior to the twin Confederate defeats at Gettysburg and Vicksburg.[61]

White, who had a reputation as an efficient administrator, went to work, quickly dividing the state into five districts in order to produce positive results for the army. District One encompassed the panhandle area, west of the Apalachicola River; Captain J.D. Westcott commanded the district. District Two was located between the Apalachicola and Suwannee Rivers. Captain Alonzo B. Noyes was in command here.

Pleasant W. White was known as an efficient administrator and, as such, received the rank of major in the Confederate army, serving as chief commissary for the state of Florida. In this role, he divided the state into five districts, in an attempt to speed the collection of cattle for delivery to Confederate armies. *State Archives of Florida.*

Suwannee, Columbia, Baker, Bradford, Nassau, Duval and Clay Counties made up District Three. This commissary district was under the command of Major Joseph P. Baldwin. Major A.G. Summer commanded the eight counties making up north and central Florida as District Four. District Five comprised major cattle country. The counties of Hernando, Hillsborough, Manatee, Polk, Brevard, Dade and Monroe were vital to the success of the program in Florida and needed an experienced hand in control. Captain James McKay ultimately provided this guidance.[62]

With his new districts in place, White had to begin calling on them immediately. He was already beginning to receive specific requests. Colonel Joseph D. Locke, the chief commissary in Georgia, estimated that Florida would need to supply a minimum of one thousand head of cattle per week to feed the troops of General Bragg and those stationed at Charleston.[63]

The situation in the field was becoming desperate, and on August 25, 1863, General Bragg wrote to Major White describing the critical nature of meat shortages and requesting any assistance possible. White replied that his goal was to ship a minimum of one thousand head per week. He leaned into his district administrators, requesting between six thousand and eight thousand heads be acquired and shipped north to Georgia. Despite evidence to the contrary, Commissary General Northrup tried to minimize the appearance of a shortage, stating that peasants in Europe rarely ate meat, and the people of Hindustan did not eat beef at all.[64]

Officers and soldiers in the field had little understanding of the difficulties faced in procuring and shipping cattle. Major John E. Cummings, based in Atlanta, was a leading critic, believing that White and his men were not making full efforts to secure the needed beef. His men in Florida claimed there were plenty of cattle available, "but the people are indisposed to sell them for our currency and drivers cannot be found."[65]

Cummings made application and received permission to send his own men into Florida to secure cattle. He quickly learned the difficulties that White had been facing. Cummings realized he needed more men and the cooperation of cattle owners, neither of which was quickly coming. Now, White was more easily able to defend his difficult position. Multiple Confederate armies were demanding cattle, cattle that were primarily located in the southern portion of the state. This issue of geography led to delays in delivering cattle fit for slaughter. Along the long trail north, drivers encountered lack of water, lack of food, poisonous snakes and difficult terrain, all of which led to long drive times, worn herds and short tempers.[66]

Despite all efforts, the requests for Florida beef continued to come in. In October, a plea from Major Henry C. Guerin, chief commissary officer for South Carolina, stated, "Our situation is full of danger…from want of meat, and extraordinary efforts are required to prevent disaster." The chief commissary of Georgia, Major M.B. Millen, wrote warning of imminent

This postwar image depicts what a cattle drive would have looked like. The men on horses are driving the cattle toward market, all the while making sure the heads eat along the way in order to keep their strength and weight up. *State Archives of Florida.*

collapse, "Starvation stares the Army in the face…I have exhausted the beef cattle, and am now obliged to kill stock cattle."[67]

Tempers were clearly running short as competing armies leaned on the overburdened White for beef. After persistent pressures, White fired back, reminding them that he had no ability to predict the massing of troops around Atlanta and thus the increased demand. He explained his own attempts to deal with shortages, stating that he had "ridden through mud and water by day and night among alligators and insects" to try to speed collections. His personal frustrations rising, White then wrote to Richmond inquiring why district commanders in Georgia had received promotion to the rank of major but those in Florida had not: "I suppose the reasons for the promotion could be equally applicable to those in this state."[68]

When the anticipated cattle were not forwarded immediately, General Bragg, whose army was hungry, began complaining directly to authorities in Richmond. The reply was not what he might have hoped. Northrup promptly reminded Bragg it was his army that abandoned the fertile lands of Tennessee. Northrup suggested if Bragg's men were hungry, they should reoccupy Tennessee and live off the fertile lands there. Bragg's situation suffered further due to a lack of suitable rail in the area, hampering delivery of any livestock being shipped his way. His men were further dejected due to unfounded rumors that millions of pounds of beef and pork were bypassing them and being delivered to the Army of Northern Virginia, under the command of Robert E. Lee.[69]

Despite the complaints from the field, numbers show that White and his agents did an admirable job under difficult circumstances in 1863. A review of District Four for the year shows shipments to Charleston of 5,679 head, 899 to Savannah and 3,564 to the Army of Tennessee. White estimated 30,000 head of cattle were legally shipped out of Florida during the year.[70]

Anticipation for cattle deliveries in 1864 did not provide for an increase in meat rations. The Army of Tennessee was then under the command of General Joseph E. Johnston, who had replaced Bragg on December 16. With an unfillable order for twenty thousand head of cattle coming from Johnston's army, White agreed the state must provide something: "The cattle will arrive in bad condition, yet I do not see how I can get along without them…We must continue the supply no matter how poor or how bad is their condition."[71]

Johnston proved himself short tempered, having to rely on "three majors in each state, none of whom owed him obedience." Johnston wanted the responsibility for acquiring food for his troops to be his, rather than that of lower level officers "who had not been thought by the government competent to the duties of high military grades."[72] Historian Robert A. Taylor has taken Johnston to task for his comments: "Johnston's remarks, besides being unkind, showed an unusual lack of tact for a man in his position. The officers he thought so deficient held the fate of his army in their hands.…Orders to continue driving until Christmas showed a poor understanding of winter condition and their effect on cattle operations on the Florida peninsula." Taylor softened his criticism, however, adding, "The general's outburst may only reflect the frustrations of a proud man losing a war."[73]

As for soldiers fighting further north, the Battle of Olustee affected them as well. There can be little doubt that one of the reasons for the failed Union action in February 1864 was to disrupt the cattle being driven north into Georgia. The action was not only a Union military loss but also led to Union prisoners of war being further deprived of rations. Confederate troops in South Carolina were receiving a short ration of beef only four out of every ten days.[74]

The forces against White increased through 1864. In addition to the travails faced in 1863, he now had to deal with the increased presence of the Union army and navy and a worsening home front that often consisted of deserters and draft evaders, unruly cattle owners and speculators and a growing pro-Union movement.

While working against these forces, White had a heated exchange with Major Guerin, the commissary agent of South Carolina. When asked as to the number of cattle he anticipated being able to supply monthly, White replied, estimating three to five hundred as his best guess. If all went well, he hoped to ship up to one thousand head. For Guerin, however, this was not satisfactory. Guerin was facing pushback on two fronts. First, the troops were hungry, and there was seldom meat to issue in rations. The second concern was socially based. There was growing discord between the classes in Charleston. The city's poor grumbled that they were living on short rations while the wealthy were occasionally able to add beef or pork to their diets. In an attempt to quell

General Joseph E. Johnston expressed considerable frustration with those in Florida attempting to provide cattle to Confederate troops. Being far from the state and not having firsthand information, Johnston did not understand the logistical issues faced by those tasked with feeding his troops. *Library of Congress.*

potential unrest, Guerin requested the Confederate government supply him with three thousand head of cattle per month, beginning as quickly as possible.

Already under strain from Richmond and various field generals, Major White snapped. Believing this request to be a direct order from Major Guerin, he angrily shot back that he took his orders from the commissary general in Richmond and that "no general [apparently referring to General Beauregard] can command me, and I will obey no orders except from those to whom I report." Realizing his request had angered the one person he most relied upon, Guerin quickly apologized, seeking to clarify that he meant his comments as a question and request only, not a direct order. White, in accepting the explanation, reiterated that three to five hundred head per month was his best estimate.[75]

As the forces working against White and his men increased in 1864, it became apparent that something had to be done in order to protect these men. James McKay, the District Five commander, was perhaps most vocal, stating in a letter to Major White, "The government is certainly very blinded in their interests in leaving the country as they do."[76] He then went further, writing to Confederate secretary of war James A. Seddon proposing a unit of soldiers who would help protect cattle herds and the men purchasing the cattle. White and his commanders determined a force of at least three hundred men was needed. These men were to be organized in a manner similar to cavalry and would be equipped to defend themselves and the cattle.

A formal request to create this group was submitted to Richmond and received a favorable audience. Upon approval, there came the important decision as to who would lead this new group. President Jefferson Davis handpicked Charles J. Munnerlyn.[77]

Munnerlyn was born in South Carolina in 1822 and enlisted in the First Georgia Volunteers, with whom he saw action in West Virginia and Florida. In 1862, the state of Georgia elected him to the Confederate House of Representatives, a position he held for only one term, losing a reelection bid in 1864. After his electoral defeat, Munnerlyn had eyes on a position as a military judge but was tapped for a major's commission and command of the First Battalion, Florida Special Cavalry, better known as the Cow Cavalry.[78]

Major Munnerlyn arrived in Florida during the spring with the daunting task of putting together his battalion. What Munnerlyn found upon his arrival was a lack of men of military age and ability. The majority had either volunteered or been conscripted into service. Munnerlyn's first achievement was appointing Captain William Footman as his executive officer. Footman was an experienced cavalry officer, having commanded Company F of the First Florida Cavalry.[79]

Munnerlyn sought out the assistance of General Joseph E. Johnston of the Army of Tennessee. Johnston's men were consistently deprived of meat in their rations, and the general was persuaded to detach some Florida natives to this new service in hopes of increasing the supply of beef.

Not just any soldier was qualified to be a member of the Cow Cavalry. Ranch hands and those with experience working with cattle were best suited to the work. In total, sixty soldiers were removed from the front lines to assist in the flatlands of Florida. Munnerlyn would be required to raise the remaining force from those men still on the home front.

The advantages of raising troops locally outweighed the disadvantages. While some of the men still in Florida may have been ill, deserters or draft dodgers, the majority were ranchers who were exempt from conscription. Volunteering for this service allowed them to remain exempt from regular army service, a role that would take them far from their homes. These volunteers had already seen, up close and personally, the need to protect their homes and families from Union troops. This familial connection helped guarantee their loyalty. Family bonds were stronger than bonds to the Confederacy. Furthermore, these men were familiar with their surroundings, providing an advantage in moving cattle and should there be fighting. In total, Munnerlyn was able to raise nine companies of soldiers throughout the year.[80]

Cow Cavalry companies went into the field beginning in April 1864. Some companies—such as Company A, under the command of Captain John T. Leslie—took quite aggressive action, including a skirmish outside of Brooksville where several soldiers were killed, and Leslie was injured.[81]

Captain Francis A. Hendry commanded Company B, a company dispatched to the southwest area of the state. Generally, Hendry's men drove small herds of cattle, usually three hundred head or less. Company C—led by the Reverend Leroy G. Leslie, father of John T. Leslie of Company A—patrolled the area around Tampa. The elder Leslie was a preacher at the First Methodist Church of Tampa, a prominent slaveholder and a veteran of the Third Seminole War. Rev. Leslie's men suffered defeat at the hands of approximately four hundred Union forces during the Brooksville Raid.[82]

The central area of the state provided two companies of men in an effort to assist in the driving of cattle. Captain W.B. Watson enlisted nearly one hundred men from the Mellonville area into Company D. Watson was an experienced soldier, having served in the Second Florida Infantry during 1862. Watson's men were "experts in their profession and absolutely indispensable," according to Major White. Watson's command was to be short lived, however, after a spy led the company into an ambush, and Watson and four others were taken prisoner while near Enterprise on Lake Monroe. Lieutenant W.B. Allen received command of the company, and the men moved to Orlando. Captain Samuel Agnew raised men who formed Company E, based out of Hodge Ferry on the Withlacoochee River.[83]

Captain Francis A. Hendry commanded troops in Company B of the First Battalion, Florida Special Cavalry, better known today as the Cow Cavalry. The role of the Cow Cavalry was to assist and protect both cattle and herders as the valuable herds were marched north to be shipped to troops in the field. *State Archives of Florida.*

Action was hot in the bend area of northern Florida. It was here that Captain James Faulkner and his men of Company F patrolled Taylor and Lafayette Counties, often fighting with the Taylor County Independent Union Rangers. The Rangers were a well-organized group of Unionists and Confederate deserters led by W. Strickland. Confederates captured Strickland and executed him, proving that Cow Cavalry duty was not for the faint of heart.[84]

Madison County, along the Florida-Georgia border, provided troops under the command of Captain J.C. Wilcox. Wilcox and Company G were tasked with providing critical protection to the rail lines that helped carry cattle heading north to the front lines for slaughter. Wilcox's men often served alongside those of Company F in protecting the Gulf Coast west of the Suwannee River, an area heavy in Union sympathy.[85]

Second Seminole War veteran and former member of the Fifth Florida Infantry William J. Bailey raised Company H from the Jefferson and Leon County areas. Command quickly passed to Captain E.A. Fernandez. Bailey and Fernandez were never able to recruit as successfully as many of the others, and Company H often worked in tandem with the men of Faulkner's or Wilcox's companies. Company G also spent time working under the overall command of General James Patton Anderson of the regular Confederate army.[86]

It was in December 1864 that Captain E.J. Lutterloh raised the final company of Cow Cavalry. Lutterloh raised less than fifty men, and he and his ragged band helped protect cattle from south Florida that stopped to graze in the Payne's Prairie area, near Gainesville.[87]

The Cow Cavalry battalion was short-lived, only remaining active until January 9, 1865. It was then that Major White was relieved of command and troops placed under General William Miller, who commanded the state troops. The commissary bureau would now have to request troops to aid in the collection and protection of cattle.[88]

Cow Cavalry troops under Captain Lutterloh met a much larger force of Union troops in February 1865 in Levy County. They skirmished over several days, alongside a force of men commanded by J.J. Dickison. The engagement ended with Union troops retreating toward Cedar Key. Union troops took with them one hundred head of cattle and an estimated fifty slaves. Dickison would later claim eighty Union casualties; the Union reports claimed six killed and eighteen wounded.[89]

Perhaps the greatest participation of Cow Cavalry came during the Battle of Fort Myers. Fort Myers was a Union military post containing "a hospital, commissary building, barracks, bakehouse, wharf, and two guardhouses, all of which were surrounded by pickets and earthworks. Many of the structures remained from Seminole War days, while others were constructed by the new occupants."[90] It was from here that Union troops raided the countryside for cattle. These cattle were driven to Punta Rassa, where they were loaded on Union blockading ships. These raids accomplished two things: they supplied meat to Union forces, and perhaps more importantly, they prevented these cattle from reaching the badly supplied Confederate forces.

During the second week of February, the recently promoted Major Footman led a force estimated at 250 on the 140-mile trek from Tampa to Fort Myers. Footman's men included the companies of John Leslie and Francis Hendry, led by James McKay Jr. Arriving at Fort Thompson on the night of February 19, they planned to leave their supply train there in anticipation of making a surprise attack on the twenty-first.[91]

Conditions in the early morning hours of February 20 proved brutal, as recounted by Lieutenant Francis Boggess: "It rained until the water was knee deep over the entire country." Despite the difficult conditions that hampered the Confederate advance, the rebels were able to capture several Union pickets from the Second Florida Cavalry (Union). Continuing their drive toward the fort, they came across a pond that Union soldiers used to wash clothes. Here, the Confederates captured five men and killed a Black sergeant.[92]

The Confederates continued their march toward the fort. Whether there was an element of surprise is unclear. Some accounts state their arrival was unexpected, while Union captain James Doyle, 110th New York Infantry, claimed the invaders were seen ahead of time and that the garrison was "instantly under arms and posted."[93]

In a change of plans, Major Footman did not immediately attack the fort. Under a flag of truce, Footman sent a surrender demand, giving the Union forces twenty minutes to accept. As the Confederate courier approached the fort, Captain John F. Bartholf of the Second United States Colored Troops met him and delivered the message to Captain Doyle, who immediately refused the demand.[94]

At 1:10 p.m., Major Footman and the Confederate forces opened fire from a distance of approximately 1,400 yards. Captain Doyle estimated that the Confederates fired only twenty shells. Union Captain Dewey of the Second United States Colored Troops commanded the Union artillery, which returned an accurate barrage. Captain Doyle's after-action report stated that the Confederates were forced to move three times during the brief exchange. The next morning, when Doyle examined the skirmish line, he found the Confederates had retreated during the night. Doyle was quick to praise his subordinates while reminding his superior officers his men were short on supplies: "I only regret that I did not have a cavalry force sufficient strong to follow them. I take this opportunity to bring to the notice of the commanding general the condition of the arms of the colored troops at this post. In both companies there are not seventy five serviceable muskets."[95]

After looking over the results of the skirmish, Captain Doyle reported that "on surveying the ground where their battery was posted bandages, splints, lint, and hastily constructed litters have been found; also pieces of wearing apparel covered with blood, which seems to show that they suffered from our fire." On the Confederate side, Lieutenant Boggess's appraisal was not complimentary of command leadership: "The whole thing had been a failure and with no bread or anything to eat but beef and parched corn. The whole command was demoralized." In addition, he credited the poor weather for "saving the lives of many" and asserted that even if the attack had been successful, it "would have had no effect on the result of the war."[96]

By mid-January 1865, the shipping of cattle from Florida had effectively come to a halt. Historian Robert A. Taylor describes two primary reasons for the stoppage. The first was the Union army, led by William T. Sherman. Its advance through and positioning in Georgia interrupted communication lines, blocked or destroyed travel routes and generally made the transport of cattle impossible. The second reason was the issue of cattle needing to forage during the trek north. During the winter months, there was not enough for cattle to eat on the route, leading to weakened herds not fit for slaughter. While some cattle traffic picked up during the spring, the numbers were inconsequential in relation to the need.

Estimates are that by the close of the war, Florida shipped more than seventy-five thousand head of cattle to the Confederate government. An untold number of cattle were sold illegally, some of them run through the blockade to countries such as Cuba. Despite never living up to the unrealistic expectations of field commanders and politicians in Richmond, Florida beef was oftentimes the only protein Confederate soldiers in the field and Union prisoners of war received. Florida beef could not stave off what eventually became inevitable defeat, but it did help prolong the fight.[97]

Chapter 4

VOLUSIA COUNTY

Volusia County is now a thriving and rapidly growing area, but most Southerners of the 1850s and 1860s would have considered it to be at the ends of the earth. In 1860, the United States Census recorded only 1,158 persons residing in the county. There were thirty-eight slaveholders with holdings totaling 297 persons. The county was heavily agricultural, and the census reports no manufacturing. Sixty-two farms are recorded in census documents. The vast majority of these were small farms, with only ten documented as 50 acres or more. A single farm is recorded over 1,000 acres. In total, only 3,008 acres of land were recorded as being improved.[98]

During the 1860 special election to elect delegates to attend the Secession Convention, Volusia County voters elected James H. Chandler, a Methodist Episcopal minister, to represent them. Chandler was originally from South Carolina and, in 1860, lived with his wife and five children in Enterprise, near the home of Captain Jacob Brock, who on the same census is shown as the owner of the steamboat *Darlington*. The Chandlers were not extremely wealthy for the time but were certainly considered comfortable. The family had real estate holdings of $350 and a personal estate of $4,250. Chandler dutifully served in his elected position, and he signed his name to the secession document.[99]

Despite the small size of the county and paucity of available men to serve, the county provided its share to the Confederate cause. Early enlistees were most likely to be members of Company H, Second Florida Infantry or Company B, Third Florida Infantry, better known as the St. Augustine Blues. Both the Second and Third Infantry regiments saw action in major battles. Unfortunately, we do not have a complete and accurate record of all men from Volusia County who served during the war.[100]

Noted Florida Civil War historian David J. Coles valuably points out that areas of seemingly minor importance, such as Volusia County, when added together across the sphere of the Confederacy, had a strong multiplier effect. Small skirmish defeats, Union control of once freely navigable rivers, deaths of friends and relatives in far-off locations and meager food supplies led to a defeatist attitude not just on the home front but also among soldiers in the field. Volusia County, remote from the major fields of battle, still played a role, albeit a minor one, during and after the Civil War.[101]

Mosquito Inlet and New Smyrna

With its eastern edge located directly on the Atlantic Ocean, and containing the tempting Mosquito Inlet, Volusia County served as an excellent entrance and exit point for blockade runners seeking to break through and deliver much-needed goods into and out of the state. Mosquito Inlet is known by the much more tourism friendly moniker of Ponce Inlet today. The inlet has always been considered hazardous, and there are dozens of stories regarding the loss of life and property associated with the currents, wind patterns and highly irregular and changing sea bottom associated with the inlet. It is by no means easy to navigate even today, and during the Civil War, it took a brave captain to sail through the area.[102]

When the Civil War began, New Smyrna was home to less than thirty families. To the north lay Mosquito Inlet and the Halifax River. To the south was Mosquito Lagoon and, ultimately, the Indian River. It is important to remember that the name of the town was New Smyrna and not New Smyrna Beach, as it is known today.

New Smyrna was in the inland settlement. Later in the 1800s, beachside land owned by Foster G. Austin became the town of Coronado Beach. The beachside community was located approximately one mile from present day Flagler Avenue. The story of the name change happened over time. In 1937, the United States Postal Service officially added Beach to the growing town's name. Nearly a decade later, in May 1945, the towns of Coronado Beach and New Smyrna Beach voted on a referendum for the two small communities to merge under the name New Smyrna Beach. Both

During the Civil War, the Sheldon family operated a hotel located atop these coquina ruins in New Smyrna. In 1863, the Union navy shelled the small town, destroying the hotel and chasing the family into the wilderness west of town. *Library of Congress.*

communities approved the measure, and on April 1, 1946, Coronado Beach officially merged into New Smyrna Beach. A seemingly embittered former mayor, James G. Schauwecker, was to say years later, "Water and electric for Coronado came from New Smyrna. Actually, we gave the town away to get New Smyrna water over here."

For visitors to New Smyrna Beach today, a favorite stop is Old Fort Park. It is located in the downtown area, and archaeologists and historians have never completely explained the ruins here. The prevailing belief is they were originally part of the construction of a manor house built during the Turnbull Settlement era. During the Civil War, John and Jane Sheldon operated a hotel atop the coquina relic. Nearby were the remains of another Turnbull-era creation, the old stone wharf. Having navigable water, a usable wharf and access both north and south, Mosquito Inlet was important for Confederate forces and their supporters.

As the Anaconda Plan tightened around Southern shipping lanes, Florida and Mosquito Inlet became the focus of more attention from both sides. Confederates needed a place to deliver supplies such as food, clothes and

This marker commemorates both the Turnbull-era stone wharf and the Civil War skirmish that occurred here in 1862. Confederate forces ambushed a small contingent of Union navy men, killing eight and wounding numerous others. *Author's photo.*

guns. Blockade runners smuggled these supplies in under cover of darkness, there being no lighthouse in the area at the time. Florida Confederates moved these goods north, often using rivers as the primary mode of transportation. Union forces sought to seize these cargoes, not only as a way to supplement their own stores but also to deprive Confederates on the battlefield.

It was in November 1861 that the steamer *Gladiator* left England loaded with guns and powder in support of the Confederacy. Union officials knew of this transport but were unsure of its destination. It was believed that Cedar Key was the most likely landing port. The steamer docked in Nassau on December 9. Confederate secretary of war Judah P. Benjamin was well aware of the shipment and hired John Fraser and Company to arrange transport of the cargo through Mosquito Inlet. Benjamin knew this was a dangerous task and summoned Robert E. Lee for help. Lee ordered General J.H. Trapier to arrange for two Parrott guns to be transported south.[103]

Lee's order read as follows:

COOSAWHATCHIE, S. C.,
January 17, 1862.

General J. H. TRAPIER,
Commanding in Florida:

GENERAL: Arrangements have been made for running into Musquito Inlet, on the east coast of Florida, arms and ammunition, by means of small fast steamers. The department considers it necessary that at least two moderate sized guns be placed at New Smyrna, to protect the landing in the event of our steamers being chased by the enemy's gunboats. You are therefore desired to send temporarily to New Smyrna some defense of this kind as soon as possible. The cargoes of the steamers are so valuable and so vitally important, that no precaution should be omitted. It will also be necessary to act very promptly, as it is hoped the steamers (two) will arrive within ten or fifteen days.

There are two Parrott guns at Fernandina, if nothing better and more available are at hand, that could be sent to the waters of the Saint John's, and thence as near the desired point as practicable, with ammunition, &c., under an active officer, with their complement of men, &c. But the guns, way, and means are left to your better knowledge and judgment.

I have the honor, &c.,
R. E. LEE,
General, Commanding.[104]

By early March, shipments were arriving via the *Kate* and *Cecil*. The vessels did not stay long and later delivered additional arms to Charleston. It was during this same period that Union troops were making their way south through the state.

On March 17, the *Penguin* arrived off the coast of Mosquito Inlet under the command of Acting Lieutenant Thomas A. Budd. Flag Officer Samuel F. Du Pont further ordered Acting Master Samuel W. Mather to take his ship the *Henry Andrew* and report to Lieutenant Budd. The job of Budd and Mather was to make a reconnaissance of the area, blockade the inlet, capture any Confederate vessels they might find and secure and ship north a load of live oak timber.[105]

Unknown to the Union forces, two companies of Confederate troops were located at New Smyrna: Companies E and H of the Third Florida Infantry, under the command of Captain Daniel E. Bird and Captain Mathew H. Strain, respectively.

During the early morning hours of March 22, 1862, Budd and Mather led a band of forty-three men and an African American guide in six rowboats south past New Smyrna. The lightly armed men were equipped with a small howitzer and several muskets. The Union men rowed south past the Sheldon Hotel and the wharf and continued toward what today are the towns of Edgewater and Oak Hill. They found an abandoned schooner, ate their dinner and slowly returned north, having encountered no enemy troops. They had no reason to anticipate strong opposition.

During the return journey, Captains Budd and Mather made the fateful decision to stop at the Turnbull-era wharf. According to Rudolphus Swift Sheldon, son of Jane and John Sheldon, there was a shed located near the

In March 1862, Flag Officer Samuel F. Du Pont ordered Union naval forces to blockade Mosquito Inlet and capture any Confederate vessels they found. In carrying out these orders, the Union navy stumbled into a Confederate ambush, costing eight lives. *Library of Congress.*

wharf that may have contained arms and ammunition. How the Union troops would know this is unexplained by Sheldon.[106]

When the boat containing both Budd and Mather pulled close to the shore, Captain Bird and his Confederates surprised the Union men. As the Union forces tried to retreat from shore, Captain Bird fired, killing Budd and others and wounding several additional men. During the skirmish, Confederates killed Acting Master Samuel Mather and injured others. The Confederates took several men prisoner. The skirmish was a rousing success for the Confederate forces. In total, eight Union men were killed, and thirty were reported injured. The Confederates captured several men, including a runaway slave serving as a guide, who was hanged. There were no reports of Confederate casualties.[107]

The following day, rowboats from the *Henry Andrew* picked up men who had not been able to return to the main ships. A rowboat went further toward New Smyrna under a flag of truce to retrieve the bodies of officers Budd and Mather. The bodies were returned, "and the commanding officer, a Captain Bird, who had come from a camp at a distance, made some show of courtesy by returning papers and a watch, as if ashamed of this mode of warfare, for these were the very troops that, with sufficient force, mean, and material for a respectable defense had ingloriously fled from St. Augustine on our approach."[108]

After suffering this tragic loss, the remaining crews of the *Penguin* and *Henry Andrew* continued on blockade duty. Misfortune continued to follow the *Henry Andrew*; the ship ran aground in April, necessitating considerable effort to free it. While Union troops were extricating the ship, Confederates took advantage of the distraction and set fire to valuable live oak and cedar logs that lay hidden along the riverbanks. Before Union troops were able to extinguish the fire, over thirty thousand feet of lumber was destroyed. Union forces located a group of approximately sixty Confederates in the area, fired on them and dispersed them to the woods.[109]

In May, Du Pont relieved the crews of the P*enguin* and the *Henry Andrew*, replacing them with the *Wyandotte*. In July, the *South Carolina* took up blockade duty with the promise from Rear Admiral Du Pont that "I will relieve you in a reasonable time."[110] The *South Carolina* was to remain at Mosquito Inlet through September, when it and its crew would depart for the state of South Carolina. For what seem to be unknown reasons, Samuel Du Pont did not send a replacement, leaving the inlet open to blockade runners.

It was not until early 1863 that the inlet was guarded regularly again. In February, the crew of the *Sagamore* was alerted that Union navy ships were again regularly patrolling Mosquito Inlet. Activity in the area became more frequent, and over the next few months, several Confederate ships, including the *Charm*, *Enterprise* and *Florence Nightingale*, were captured.

During July 1863, the Union ships *Beauregard*, *Sagamore*, *Para* and *Oleander* met outside of Mosquito Inlet. Here the *Oleander*, a shallow drafted vessel, began to tow the larger *Beauregard* through the inlet before it ran aground. The *Oleander* continued further south before anchoring in the river near the Sheldon Hotel.

In the words of Rudolphus Swift Sheldon,

> *At flood tide, when the vessels swung around, presenting their broadsides to the house, without a word of warning, they opened fire on it and on the Carpenter House, with long parrot shells. It was twelve o'clock noon, we had not eaten*

dinner, which was on the range cooking. At the first crash of shells through the house we all fled to the woods. Two hours afterwards came one of the hardest showers I ever experienced and drenched us to the skin. The boats ceased firing during the shower and I stole up to the house by the rear entrance, and succeeded in packing up enough food to last us two days. They opened fire again, while I was in there, and a shell came through the parlor but a few feet from me, and sliced off the top of our piano as nicely as though cut with a knife. They continued shelling all night, and in the morning sent a party to shore, which burned all that was left of both houses.[111]

The official report submitted by Lieutenant Commander Earl English is similar but contains enough differences to allow for questioning of Sheldon's story.

The Oleander took the Beauregard in tow, crossed the bar, and anchored abreast the place, giving it a good shelling, the boats going up past the town. We captured one sloop loaded with cotton, one schooner not laden; caused them to destroy several vessels, some of which were loaded with cotton and about ready to sail. They burned large quantities of it on shore, which we could not prevent. Landing a strong force, destroyed all the buildings that had been occupied by troops. In landing, the party was fired upon by a number of stragglers concealed in the bushes. The conduct of all connected with the expedition was most praiseworthy.[112]

With this action, Confederate blockade running into New Smyrna slowed considerably. Several blockading ships rotated through the Mosquito Inlet area during the last years of the war, but little action was to be found. Historian Thomas Graham succinctly closes the book on blockade running at Mosquito Inlet: "What happened at Mosquito Inlet was repeated elsewhere along the South's seacoast, and eventually the blockade substantially reduced the Confederacy's ability to continue the war."[113]

John Milton and Esther Hawks, Freemanville and Hawks Park

Born in Bradford, New Hampshire, on November 28, 1826, to Colburn and Clarissa Hawks, John Milton Hawks—Milton, as he was commonly called—exhibited a thirst for knowledge at an early age. Encouraged by his parents,

John Milton Hawks was an abolitionist and surgeon during the Civil War. Hawks served as assistant surgeon to the Thirty-Third United States Colored Troops and later surgeon to the Twenty-First USCT. After the war, he formed a lumber company that provided jobs to more than five hundred Black soldiers. He later founded the city of Hawks Park, now known as Edgewater, Florida. *State Archives of Florida.*

Milton completed his early education at age sixteen and became a teacher. Hawks was to resign his teaching job and pursue further education in medicine, and after several starts and stops, he received his MD from Cincinnati, Ohio–based Eclectic Medical College in 1847.

While preparing to open his medical practice, Hawks became very ill and thus dependent on his sister Helen for care. The young doctor recuperated, later stating, "I was not afraid to die. But didn't want to, so I didn't."[114] In the fall of 1848, Hawks went into partnership with a Dr. Collins, joining a successful practice. His professional success coupled with his belief in favor of women's suffrage made him a highly prized bachelor. In 1850, he was introduced to Esther Hill, who was almost eight years his junior.

Esther Hill was born to a family with a legacy of participation in the American Revolution and War of 1812. She was born to Parmenas and Jane Hill on August 5, 1833. She excelled in school in an era when education for girls was not normally encouraged. Esther and Milton were married on October 5, 1854. The newly wedded Hawkses honeymooned in Florida, where they both fell in love with the state. Milton was attracted to the opportunities in the citrus industry, while Esther found a short-term teaching position at a Methodist Church, teaching African American children. Esther also took an interest in Milton's work and immersed herself in his medical texts.

Upon returning to New Hampshire in 1855, the Hawkses reopened Milton's medical practice, along with a drug store. Esther was still interested in medicine and enrolled in the New England Female Medical College, located in Boston. Two years later, she was to graduate as part of a seven-member class.

Sectional tensions were escalating, and the Hawkses were known abolitionists. Milton had gone so far as to write, "Let us liberate the slaves, take them into our service and place weapons in their hands….Let us join the war for the Union and the Constitution, and make it also a War of Emancipation.…Let us once more unfurl the Stars and Stripes over all the territory.…And when our banner shall again float in the Southern breeze, the sons of Africa will no longer curse it, for not a slave shall be left shackled beneath its folds."[115]

Answering the call of war, Milton was to join the Freedmen's Aid Association, while Esther attempted to become an army physician or nurse. Dorothea Dix turned down Esther's application; Dix wanted to hire middle-aged, plain-looking women only. Milton was sent to South Carolina, where he served as superintendent in charge of the Union-controlled plantation at Edisto Island. Esther joined him in the fall of 1862. She soon began work with one other woman as a teacher, attempting to educate more than three hundred men, women and children.

While living in South Carolina, Milton volunteered for service, receiving the rank of major in the United States Army. At Milton's urging, a regiment of African Americans was mustered into service in October 1862. It was not until April 1863, however, that General Hospital No. 10 was opened. This hospital was created to treat injured Black soldiers, who were not welcomed at White hospitals. Both Milton and Esther worked at No. 10. In addition to her medical duties, "Miz Hawk," as her students called her, continued to teach regularly.

As would be expected, Milton was moved regularly in the line of duty, with Esther often accompanying him. In 1864, the Hawkses found themselves in Florida because of the Battle of Olustee. Here, in the ruggedness of northern Florida, both Milton and Esther cared for the wounded, Black and White. While stationed in Florida, Esther continued her teaching duties, including operating an integrated school in the Jacksonville area in late 1864.

As the war drew to its merciful close, their prior owners, more often than not, abandoned former slaves. Often these people—just recently considered pieces of property to be sold at will—had no food, no home, no clothing and little hope for a better life. Esther went back to work, creating an orphanage and forming schools. She received appointment as the general superintendent of schools in the area. Because of the condition the former slaves had been kept in, these new schools taught a wide range of skills. In addition to traditional subjects, the students also received direction in life skills that would help them as they adjusted to their newly received freedom.

In the postwar years, Milton desired to return to Florida, a land of opportunity he fondly remembered. He was a founding member of the Florida Land and Lumber Company, serving as president. In addition to his role in the fledgling lumber company, he purchased five hundred acres of land that had been a part of the Geronimo-Alvarez Grant for the then high price of one dollar per acre. These acres were to be the genesis of Hawks Park.

Despite her concerns over the financial wellbeing of the company, Esther left the area, returning to Charleston, where she received appointment to a leadership position dealing with quartermaster stores. Here, she helped provide supplies to those in need, particularly the freedmen. She was also able to keep her hands involved in the schools she had recently formed.

Milton began work in Florida, creating the community named Port Orange. As Milton later said, "I chose the name of Port Orange because there was no other Port Orange Post Office in the United States. So if a person forgot to add the state on the envelope, it would come to Florida."[116] The goal in creating Port Orange was "to secure homesteads for Freedmen and others, and to furnish a profitable investment for capital."[117] Milton himself would later say, "The original design of the community was to start a colony of freedmen and those who could be friendly to them on the public lands near the Mosquito Inlet. Homesteads were secured on the north side of Spruce Creek and at Dun-Lawton and at one time 500 families came here from Columbia, S.C."[118] Freemanville became the name of the new home for the freedmen working for Milton Hawks. Over the years, much of the history of this pioneering community, including the Gadsden Cemetery, has been lost.[119]

In hindsight, the Florida Land and Lumber Company was doomed from the start. The freedmen were starting from scratch. They had to clear land, construct homes and plant crops in order to feed the workers. Life for the newly arrived residents was seemingly no better than what they had left in South Carolina, and the internal grumbling began. Despite the difficulties, however, the workers were free and able to create a new life for themselves and their families.

The venture appears to have been severely underfunded and overly ambitious. A steam engine was purchased out of Bangor, Maine, necessitating a long and dangerous voyage south. Additional machinery required purchase, shipment and installation. The sawmill building itself required construction. What little funding remained was required to train employees and meet payroll obligations.

In November 1866, Esther returned to Florida in an attempt to help and provide guidance. She soon opened a school in New Smyrna that educated approximately forty students. Milton appears to have been restless, however.

He was appointed postmaster in Port Orange but also held the title of collector of customs in Pensacola, a community 450 miles away.

Hawks stopped meeting payroll in the fall of 1866, leading to the departure of most employees and their families. Reports from 1868 state that only nine of the original settling families were still at Port Orange.[120] By 1870, the Florida Land and Lumber Company had completely failed.

As reported in the *Florida Historical Quarterly*:

> *Thirty thousand dollars was pledged as stock, of which two-thirds was paid in. This was thrown away in a vain attempt to build and run a large steam saw mill. The first error was in changing its plan to have a small portable mill; and to purchase one of three times the capacity needed; and worse than that, a second hand one standing at Bangor, ME. All the company property was mortgaged to raise money to complete the mill and buy the first stock of logs. The large two story mill is still standing on the bank of the river with machinery complete but idle.[121]*

Esther again left Florida. This time, she returned to New Hampshire, where she resumed her medical practice. She and Milton would visit each other, often escaping the extremes of Florida and New England weather. Many of the freedmen also left Port Orange, seeking out better opportunities in communities such as Jacksonville or Palatka.

By 1874, Milton had put considerable effort into his new venture, Hawks Park, a community he touted as a "New England Village on the Atlantic Coast of South Florida."[122] He had finished construction on a family home consisting of four rooms spread over two stories. He further kept himself busy researching and writing several volumes containing what we now call vital statistics.

Despite Milton's successes, Esther was to remain in New England for her remaining years, moving to Lynn, Massachusetts, in 1884. She was active in charitable and philanthropic efforts and never gave up her devotion to education. Esther took ill in 1906, at the age of seventy-two, and died on May 6. She was buried in Manchester, New Hampshire. On her tombstone are words she herself chose: "On the proper training of the children, rests the hopes of the world."

John Milton Hawks was to live several more years before passing away on April 2, 1910, at the age of eighty-four. Upon hearing the news of Hawks's death, local resident Mary Jane Marshall hurried off a letter to her children, closing with, "Well I can truthfully say that one of the best men living has gone and how we are going to miss him."[123] Hawks's remains were buried in his beloved Hawks Park, now better known as Edgewater, to spend eternity far from his wife, much as he had during their marriage. A marker at his burial location notes his founding of Hawks Park, and a military stone references his service as a surgeon to the Twenty-First USCT.

Today, there is little left of the Freemanville settlement. The area formerly known as Freemanville is now a rectangle of roads just west of U.S. 1 in Port Orange, bordered on the south by West Ocean Avenue, on the west by Alexander Avenue, on the east by North Orange Avenue and on the north by Valley Street. The Mount Mariah Baptist Church is often called the last vestige of this community.[124] In 2002, the City of Port Orange erected a historic marker to the memory of Freemanville. This marker is located at the entrance to Riverwalk Park on U.S. 1.

CAPTAIN SIMMONS BENNETT

The live oak industry was, for many years, a valuable one for the Volusia County area. Live oaking involved the cutting and transport north of enormous live oak trees, whose lumber would be used to build the large sailing ships of the nineteenth century.

One of the leading families in the industry was the Swift family of New Hampshire. The Swift brothers started coming south after the War of 1812 and were well known along the east coast of Florida for their yearly winter trips. The Florida heat, insects and fear of yellow fever prevented a longer harvesting season. The brothers ran a large live oak operation. Some years, they arrived with more than five hundred men and all the needed equipment.

It was under the direction of Elijah Swift that young Simmons Bennett first came to Florida as a young man of around twenty. No doubt strong and experienced from his prior work as a shipyard apprentice in New Hampshire, the young Bennett helped with logistical work. Bennett continued to return to Florida annually, despite the regional concerns over slavery. When fighting broke out in spring 1861, the Swift operation quickly fled Florida, leaving young Simmons Bennett behind to oversee materials left after the hasty retreat. These items included boats, mules, carts and thousands of board feet of usable timber.

According to historian Ianthe Bond Hebel, the Swift yard was located at what is now the county courthouse in Daytona Beach, off Beach Street.

The live oak timber business was a profitable one, especially for the Swift brothers of New Hampshire. The large trees were felled and sent north to be used in the construction of sailing ships. This image from Seville is representative of trees that loggers found throughout Volusia County. *Library of Congress.*

Bennett was able to see firsthand the rising tensions in the state. Confederates regularly raided the Swift yard. All livestock was stolen, equipment was taken or destroyed and the Swift buildings were burned. Realizing he was in personal danger, Simmons Bennett joined the Confederate service in May

1862, serving in Company G of the Eighth Florida Infantry. His July 1862 compiled service record shows young Bennett was sent to Tallahassee Hospital with an unspecified illness. He appears to have never returned to service.

In the postwar years, Bennett returned to the area with the Swift brothers. In 1868, he again stayed in Florida after the brothers' annual return north. Here, he married Victoria Voss in July 1870. They were to be the parents of four children, three of whom lived to adulthood. Bennett appears to have earned the nickname Captain from his time operating a freight line between Port Orange and Jacksonville. It was in this role that Bennett helped provide needed supplies and food to the growing area. Through the years, Bennett and his sons built and sold numerous ships, including the *Eliza Bennett* and the *Royal Palm*. In addition to his boating skills, Bennett operated the Tourist Hotel, a rooming lodge located on South Palmetto Avenue.[125]

Despite these accolades, Bennett may be best remembered for a failure he and others encountered. In the summer of 1908, a group of nine large whales beached themselves at Coronado Beach (now a part of New Smyrna Beach). Bennett, along with local businessperson Frank Sams and others, tried to capitalize on this, attempting to extract oil from the carcasses. Their effort was a resounding failure and led to a stench hanging over the beach community for several days. Finally, the remains of the carcasses were pulled out to sea in an attempt to rid the beach of the sight and smell.[126]

Whales on beach, near New Smyrna, Fla.

Having worked as a live oaker and Confederate soldier, Simmons Bennett may be best remembered today for his attempt to extract oil from whale carcasses that washed ashore at Coronado Beach. This postcard image recreates the scene. *Author's photo.*

Captain Simmons Bennett spent the remainder of his long life in Daytona Beach before passing at the age of eighty-six in February 1924. A Confederate service headstone marks Bennett's burial site in Pinewood Cemetery in Daytona Beach, despite his service being extremely limited.

WILLIAM ROWLINSKI

In a career during which he was more known for his skills as a lighthouse keeper than as a soldier, William Rowlinski played a key role in the early history of Ponce Inlet. Born in Russia in 1833, Rowlinski immigrated to the United States at the age of seventeen. Rowlinski settled in Charleston, South Carolina, where he married Mary Jane Rebecca Hilton in 1857. William joined the Confederate army, mustering into Company A, Twenty-Fourth South Carolina Infantry. In 1864, Union forces captured and later imprisoned young Rowlinski at Camp Douglas in Chicago. After his release in 1865, the Rowlinski family settled in Salters, South Carolina, and began raising a family.

Russian immigrant William Rowlinski served in the Twenty-Fourth South Carolina Infantry before joining the Lighthouse Service. He served as the first principal keeper of the Mosquito Inlet Light Station. Private Rowlinski is buried in Edgewater-New Smyrna Cemetery. *Author's photo.*

In December 1883, William joined the Lighthouse Service, receiving appointment as second assistant keeper at the St. Augustine Light Station. As was common in this service, the Rowlinski family moved several times as William received different appointments. On December 31, 1887, Rowlinski was appointed to the coveted position of principal keeper of the new Mosquito Inlet Light Station, at a salary of $720 per year.

Rowlinski later received a transfer to the Georgetown, South Carolina, light station in 1893, where he stayed until resigning from the service in 1902. Rowlinski and his wife returned to Mosquito Inlet, where he resided until his death in 1914.

Until 2005, Private Rowlinski's remains were buried in an unmarked tomb in Edgewater New Smyrna Cemetery. That year, the Sons of Confederate Veterans unveiled a new government-issued headstone bearing notice of Rowlinski's Civil War service and his career as a lighthouse keeper.[127]

Chapter 5

THE BATTLE OF MARIANNA

T hen under the command of Brigadier General Alexander Asboth, of the Federal Military District of West Florida, lands lying west of Tallahassee (with the exception of Pensacola) were often considered remote and out of mind. In September 1864, General Asboth received information leading him to make a raid out of Pensacola toward the northeast. He wrote to Major George Drake, then the assistant adjutant general for the Department of the Gulf:

> *I have the honor to report that owing to information received and forwarded yesterday, under No. 1045, I am to start on a cavalry raid into the northeastern portion of West Florida. Going up the Santa Rosa Island and swimming the horses across the East Pass to the mainland, I will proceed to Port Washington and from thence to Marianna and vicinity, returning via Saint Andrews Salt Works. My object is to capture the isolated rebel cavalry and infantry in Washington and Jackson counties, and to liberate the Union prisoners held at Marianna, to collect white and colored recruits, and secure as many horses and mules as possible. All the infantry will remain here for the safety of Barrancas and surroundings.*[128]

Marianna was the county seat of Jackson County and home to approximately five hundred residents. The community was an isolated one, with the nearest rail lines approximately fifty miles away. While the region contributed a considerable number of men to the war effort, its isolation also made it an area known for Confederate deserters and those avoiding conscription. Also located at Marianna was a Confederate hospital under the command of assistant surgeon Henry Robinson.[129]

Asboth was correct in his statement that the area was home to Confederate cavalry. Under the command of Colonel Alexander Blair Montgomery, a former West Point graduate who came to Confederate service after a career in the private sector, were several companies detached from the Fifth Florida Battalion of Cavalry.

In writing to Major C.T. Christensen, Asboth estimated the Confederate forces around Marianna at "300 infantry (militia) and 100 cavalry" spread among several companies. He also believed that there were several hundred Union prisoners there.[130] As historian Mark F. Boyd stated, "It is not likely that any [company] had more than 75 men enrolled, and it may be expected that all were characterized more by ardor than discipline."[131]

Union troops left Fort Barrancas on September 18, 1864, headed toward Marianna. General Asboth had with him seven hundred men when they crossed Pensacola Bay, landing at Navy Cove, Live Oak Plantation. From there, the men marched fifty miles along Jackson Road to Rodgers' Gap, which was located across the narrows of Santa Rosa Island, six miles west of East Pass. It was here that Asboth was able to replenish his troops with supplies from the steamer *Lizzie Davis*.

The march continued for more than one hundred miles. On the twenty-third, they made a surprise attack on the Euchee Anna courthouse, scoring a large success, gathering up "nine prisoners of war and 6 political prisoners, 46 horses with equipments, 8 mules, and 28 stand of arms. With the prisoners [were] W.H. Terrence, militia colonel; First Lieut. Francis M. Gordon, Fifteenth Confederate Cavalry; William Cathon, an influential rebel leader; and Allen Hart, a wealthy rebel beef contractor." Asboth returned the prisoners, along with sixteen "colored recruits," to the *Lizzie Davis* for processing.[132]

Asboth continued his march on the twenty-fourth, driving toward Huett's Bluff and Cerro Gordo, located on the west bank of the Choctawhatchee River. Crossing the river on the twenty-fifth, the men continued toward Campbellton, reaching Marianna on the twenty-seventh. After "a sharp engagement," the town belonged to Union forces that afternoon. Asboth described the skirmish in his after-action report:

> *Rebel troops were constantly in close vicinity of my column, with frequent skirmishes with my vanguard, they gave us battle only at Marianna, which*

resulted in a brilliant victory for my command. The first charge upon the town, with the rebel cavalry in front formed in line of battle and the militia sharpshooters concentrated in the grave-yard, church, and other buildings on the left flank of the narrow path through which we had to pass, was repulsed. The second, however, was led by myself, was a brilliant and successful one, and all my troops except the repulsed battalion of the Second Maine Cavalry behaved with the utmost gallantry and secured for our raid a most decided success.

We captured 81 prisoners of war, 95 stand of arms, quantities of commissary and quartermaster's stores, over 200 fine horses and excellent mules, 17 wagons, and over 400 head of cattle, already brought within our lines, besides over 600 contrabands who followed us with the greatest enthusiasm. The most prominent of the rebel officers taken and already brought within our lines are Brig. Gen. William E. Anderson, of the militia, and Col. A.B. Montgomery, a West Pointer of the regular Confederate Army, commanding the District of West Florida.[133]

During the fighting, there was considerable damage to the town, and both sides suffered a number of casualties. Upon hearing of the approaching Union forces, Confederate colonel Montgomery had home guard troops put together a barricade across Lafayette Street. This barricade caused the Second Maine Cavalry trouble, as Asboth stated in his report. With the arrival of General Asboth and his flanking party, Colonel Montgomery ordered Confederate forces to retreat toward the Chipola River. Union troops captured Colonel Montgomery during this retreat.

For a small skirmish, the fighting was intense. Asboth himself received considerable injury: "I myself was also honored by the rebels with two balls, the first in the face, breaking the cheek bone, the other fracturing my left arm in two places."[134] Asboth was to leave command of his force with Colonel L.L. Zulavsky, of the Eighty-Second United States Colored Troops, who was the ranking officer.

Located in the center of the fighting, St. Luke's Episcopal Church and surrounding buildings were set ablaze. A postwar story of dubious validity relates to the modern incarnation of the church. A large nineteenth-century Bible is encased and on display at the church. Legend states that upon hearing the order to torch the church, Union officer Major Nathan Cutler of the Second Maine Cavalry ran through the flames to save the precious Bible. When he exited the church, he encountered two Southern boys, who—when Cutler refused to surrender—peppered him with shot. Despite

The Florida Division of the United Confederate Veterans held their thirty-seventh annual convention in Marianna September 26–29, 1927. Note the elderly former Confederates standing underneath the United States flag. *State Archives of Florida.*

Cutler's injuries, the Bible was preserved. Surgeon George Martin of the Second Maine tells a different version of Cutler's injuries, one which Cutler himself confirmed in a pension application.

> *I saw Major Cutler wounded at Marianna. He was charging at the head of his command down the main street when a volley was fired by the Rebs from the churchyard, making 8 wounds in the left leg, thigh and forearm. His horse fell dead, riddled with bullets. I had him taken to the mayor's house and dressed his wounds. His arm was severely fractured, and we were obliged to leave him there when we retreated the next day. I think his ankle was also broken.*

If we were to take Martin's word, it would appear obvious that Cutler received his wounds before the church was set ablaze. In a later interview, Cutler did recall a Union officer objecting to the burning of the church. If true, it was most likely that unnamed soldier, and not Cutler, who salvaged the Bible, either before or as the church burned.[135]

Union casualties were small in number but, in some cases, serious. General Asboth did not state his number of casualties, but the *West Florida News* reported fifteen killed and forty wounded. Of the wounded, six were officers. Officers suffering wounds included Majors Hutchinson and Cutler, Captain Stanley and Lieutenants Adams, Moody and Rowley. Cutler and Adams were cared for in the Confederate hospital at Marianna. Federal losses included Captain

This granite obelisk monument is dedicated to Confederate troops who held off "overwhelming federal forces" during the Battle of Marianna. More than four thousand people attended a grand dedication ceremony on November 2, 1921. *State Archives of Florida.*

M.M. Young of the Seventh Vermont, who served as Asboth's assistant adjutant general, and Lieutenant Ayer of the Second Maine.[136]

The *News* estimated Confederate losses at nine killed, sixteen wounded and fifty-four taken prisoner. Of the dead, reports claimed that four perished because of the church burning.[137] The local courthouse held Confederate prisoners; some received parole on the spot.

General Asboth was evacuated with other wounded Union soldiers and transported to Point Washington. Here, Asboth and his men set sail for Fort Barrancas aboard the *Lizzie Davis*. They docked on October 1, and Asboth was sent to New Orleans, where he was to receive additional treatment. Confederate prisoners were sent to prisons at Elmira or Fort Delaware. Five Confederates captured at Marianna were to die in these Union prisons.[138]

The Union left their dead behind to be dealt with by locals. According to historian Mark Boyd, the remains were interred in the town graveyard before being moved to Andersonville National Cemetery.[139]

The short skirmish was commemorated in 1921 with the dedication of an obelisk monument by the William Henry Milton Chapter of the Florida Division of the United Daughters of the Confederacy (UDC), the citizens of Marianna and the state legislature. The UDC raised over $1,000 and the Florida legislature appropriated $5,000.

On November 2, 1921, a dedication ceremony was held with more than four thousand people in attendance. The celebration included a parade featuring the United States Navy Band from Pensacola, National Guard units, Boy Scout troops, Confederate veterans and more. Speakers at the event included Mayor N.A. Baltzell, Dr. Theophilius West, who had served as assistant surgeon for the Eighth Florida Infantry during the Civil War, and Florida governor Cary A. Hardee.

When the time came, two young girls received the honor of unveiling the monument: the granddaughter of John Milton, the Civil War–era governor of the state, and Floie Criglar, the grandniece of General William Miller, the Confederate field general during the battle of Marianna. The McNeel Marble Company manufactured the monument, which is made of Georgia granite. The obelisk shaft stands on a pedestal base and rises thirty-six feet in the air.

The following inscription is on the west-facing side of the monument:

> *Battle of Marianna*
> *Sept. 27, 1864*
> *Where Overwhelming*
> *Federal Forces Were*
> *Stubbornly Resisted*
> *By a Home Guard of*
> *Old Men and Boys*[140]
> *And A Few Sick and*
> *Wounded Confederates*
> *on Furlough*[141]

Chapter 6

WEST FLORIDA SEMINARY CADETS

First created by the Florida legislature on January 24, 1851, and known back then as the Florida Institute, the newly named West Florida Seminary came into existence on January 1, 1857. It was originally opened as a boys' school; girls from the Tallahassee Female Academy were admitted to the Female Institute, housed in a separate building, beginning on October 1, 1858.[142]

Enrollment was never high, rising to a level of approximately 250 during the 1860–61 school year. Most other years show fewer than 100 students enrolled, combined male and female.[143] The school expanded in the postwar years and, by 1897, had evolved into the first liberal arts school in the state. The school became known as Florida State College in 1901.[144]

Despite the seemingly low enrollment, the West Florida Seminary appears to have been successful. The school building was located on the present-day spot of the Westcott Administration Building of Florida State University. The City of Tallahassee and the state seminary fund provided funding for school operations. The seminary fund provided revenue from the sale of lands donated by the federal government. The school offered education in mathematics, reading, spelling and writing for younger students. Older students studied algebra, natural science, geography, English, Greek, Latin and other subjects.[145]

As sectional tensions continued to rise, school principal Duncan Turner took the opportunity to visit several southern military schools in a fact-finding mission to see if a military-type education might be feasible in Florida. By 1860, the local paper reported that "a detachment of young cadets from the State Seminary commanded by Capt. N. W. Eppes" took part in "a fine military display" during Independence Day celebrations.[146]

The 1860–61 school year saw further change, as state legislation gave the school authorization to "organize said Seminary upon a collegiate and military basis, and to make for the government of said Institution such rules and regulation as may be necessary to carry out the provisions of this act." The West Florida Seminary Board of Education then directed the faculty to "prepare a catalogue of Studies, Rules, Regulations, &c. For the permanent organization of [the] Seminary upon a Collegiate and Military basis."[147]

In 1863, the legislature changed the name of the school yet again. With war at a fever pitch, the school was renamed Florida Military and Collegiate Institute. This was not to be a military school in name only, however. During an August 1864 board of trustees meeting, school principal V.M. Johnson wrote,

> *I then propose that the Board authorize me to secure the exemption of the school from military duty, except for those of a military age, at the discretion of the Governor or General Commanding the Department of Florida in cases of great emergency. I propose lastly, to secure additional arms and accouterments for the use of the school, uniforms for the Cadets, and indeed, to do everything that is necessary to make this school a first class Military of Academy, an honor to the Board, and the price [of] the state.*[148]

At the following meeting, on August 23, 1864, board members again discussed the subject; the minutes record the following:

> *Upon motion the following resolution was adopted—Resolved: That the President of the Board be authorized and requested, after conference with the Governor of the State, and with Captain Johnston to take measures to obtain from the authorities in Richmond permission for youths under 18 years of age to pursue their studies at the Military Academy until such emergency shall occur as to require their services in the field, under an assurance that such youths shall be armed and disciplined and held subject to any requisition for military duty.*[149]

Such an emergency would not be far in the future.

President of the Confederate States of America Jefferson Davis understood that sending boys into war out of Southern military schools was not a good long-term strategy. He referred to this as "grinding the seed corn." *Library of Congress.*

Attendance at the institute had dropped precipitously from the 250 students at the start of the war to only 58 total boys and girls for the 1864–65 school year. Thirty-four of the students were boys, with an estimated age range of eight to seventeen. This drop was most likely due to several factors. The Seminary Board was required to raise tuition in response the falling value of the Confederate dollar. In the fall of 1864, tuition for secondary students stood at $160, while the cost for primary students was $120. Books and supplies were difficult, if not impossible, to find due to war shortages and the impact of the Union embargo. A third factor affecting the school was the lack of qualified instructors and administrators. Able-bodied men were fighting on the front lines, leaving few resources available for the board to select from.[150]

The issue of using seminary and military-school-age boys as troops was a controversial one. These cadets were hardly men, let alone hardened, combat-ready fighters. As early as 1861, Confederate president Jefferson Davis had stated on the subject, "In making soldiers of them, we are grinding the seed corn."[151] Davis understood that by sacrificing these boys, who were learning military technique and theory, the Confederacy was cannibalizing future homegrown officers. Despite his preference, students from the four major military colleges of the Confederacy—Virginia Military Institute, South Carolina Military Academy, Georgia Military Institute and the University of Alabama—were called into service during crucial periods of the war.[152]

Seminary students received a call to action in early 1864, when Federal troops advanced westward from Jacksonville, culminating at Olustee. Cadet William A. Rawls recalled many years later, "All troops, including Home Guards had been sent to Olustee. All boys big enough to be allowed to go joined them, and went as part of their organization."[153]

After the Battle of Olustee, Confederate troops confined Union prisoners in Tallahassee, with Seminary students taking on the role of prison guards. Cadet Rawls further describes their service: "They did guard duty when there were no other troops available in Tallahassee, and guarded Federal prisoners in the military hospital, which is the Masonic building. I have walked post there, [as did] all other Cadets of the West Florida Seminary....Afterward, they were called upon at any time they were needed to perform military duty."[154]

It was in 1865, however, that the seminary students were most tested. In early March, Union forces landed at the St. Marks lighthouse, causing the alarm to be rung in nearby Tallahassee. Brigadier General John Newton was leading a force consisting of the Second and Ninety-Ninth United States Colored Troops along with the Second Florida Union Cavalry. In addition to the goal of damaging blockade-running operations in the area, it is highly probable that a raid on Tallahassee was part of the plan.

Major General John Newton commanded troops at the Battle of Natural Bridge, outside of Tallahassee, in 1865. Confederate forces repulsed Newton's efforts, allowing Tallahassee to remain the only Confederate capital east of the Mississippi River not to fall into Union hands. *Library of Congress.*

On March 5, Governor John Milton made a call for troops, and "every man and boy capable of bearing arms was at his post." By noon of that day, cadets from the seminary were assembled and marched to the state capital, where they "were regularly enlisted and sworn into Confederate service."[155]

Ellen Call Long, the daughter of territorial governor Richard Keith Call, recounts that the cadets "shouldered their muskets like veterans, and followed with the confidence of inexperience, which is usually more zealous than wise; but sometimes the one is needed more than the other."[156] Sue Archer, a student in the Female Institute, told an even more emotionally charged story of the cadets leaving Tallahassee:

> *Mothers and sisters went to the station to say good-bye to them. The little fellows were full of patriotism and seemed to feel no fear. One little boy barefooted and wearing the cadets' uniform stood apart from the others, and was crying; because Captain Johnson refused to let him go, as he was so young, and also because he was the only son of a poor blind woman. Captain Johnson told him that good soldiers did not cry, and that when he grew older he should go into the war.*[157]

In 1865, Confederate major general Samuel Jones served in command of the Department of Florida and South Georgia. Under his command, Confederate troops, including boys from the West Florida Seminary, repelled Union attacks at the Battle of Natural Bridge, helping keep Tallahassee the only Confederate capital east of the Mississippi River not to fall into Union hands. *Library of Congress.*

Just how many boys left on the train from Tallahassee is a point of much discussion. Several contemporaries placed the number at around sixty-five, an impossibility considering records show less than sixty boys of all ages enrolled for the semester. Historian David J. Coles has made a fine examination of this topic and has put forth an estimate of twenty-five cadets sent toward the battle. This number corresponds with the later statement of Confederate soldier J.L. Blocker, who remembered twenty to thirty cadets reinforcing his unit. The ages of these seminary cadets ranged from eleven to eighteen.[158]

The train carrying the cadets arrived at Newport on the afternoon of March 5. They found themselves immediately under fire as they looked to take up spots in a line of breastworks. While some Confederate troops moved to the area where the St. Marks River ran underground, called the Natural Bridge, the cadets remained at Newport. helping to prevent a Union incursion at that location.

Later that morning, officers ordered the cadets to march toward Natural Bridge. Along the way, they became acquainted with the real horrors of war. During the march, cadets witnessed the damage caused by Union artillery shells: pine trees in half providing evidence of their forceful nature. The boys also witnessed the body of an injured Confederate casualty being hauled from the field toward medical care in the rear.

Upon arriving on the field of battle, the boys were placed near the middle of the Confederate line, near the Kilcrease Artillery. They began digging a trench to fortify their location. While most stayed behind the relative safety of earthworks, a Confederate artilleryman recalled a story of several boys with more courage than experience.

The new issue boys were armed with old smooth, bore muskets, iron ramrod, shooting a ball and three buck shots. I was amused at four of these

boys behind a small tree, the front one with one of these muskets along side
of the tree, and the other three playing tag at his back. He fired the musket,
which kicked him back, knocking those behind him down backward. All
arose astonished; two of them ran off, and the other two stayed to reload the
musket. They did not attempt to fire it again.[159]

A secondary witness left a statement that, when taken with the above, could add up to a level of believability. A Confederate captain named Johnson recalled, "The cadets were gallant under fire, but including to be impetuous, and it was with difficulty that [he] restrained them from unnecessary risks."[160]

As the day wore on and additional Confederate reinforcements arrived, General Newton realized that Union forces would not be able to cross the St. Marks River. He reluctantly ordered a retreat toward the lighthouse and the protection of the navy fleet.

Upon the Union retreat, the cadets were ordered back to Newport should the Union try another crossing there. Confederate casualties were slight at less than thirty. The Union suffered 148 killed, wounded, captured or missing. Cadets from the seminary suffered no casualties. Susan Archer was to claim later that a young drummer by the name of Dick Frazier died from a fall off the train on the way to Newport. While this was a tragic loss, Frazier was not a cadet.[161]

Most locals accepted that the cadets from the seminary performed their duty well and showed exemplary courage. Many returned to Tallahassee, while others remained at Newport for additional service. This service included guarding two Confederate deserters and witnessing their execution. The cadets also accompanied a group of twenty-five prisoners to Tallahassee. The *Tallahassee Democrat* was quick to heap praise on the young cadets: "The cadets from the Florida State Seminary were in the fight and behaved in a most gallant manner. Their praise is on the lips of all who took part in the fight." A short time later, in an elaborate ceremony at the capital, the cadets were presented a company flag.[162]

While the praise of the cadets was almost universal, there was one instance where they were condemned. The scene when they first entered the field of battle led to one of the long-lasting controversies of the cadets' participation. In 1918, the *Tallahassee Democrat* published an editorial written by Cade E. Shackelford calling for the state to purchase the Natural Bridge Battlefield and erect an appropriate memorial there. This appeal served to greatly inflate the role played by the cadets, claiming, "The Confederate troops that so nobly and successfully defended the capital city of their state, was largely made up of boys in their teens, at the time attending school at the West Florida Seminary, the military school of the state at Tallahassee."[163]

While it might be understandable to overstate the role of boys in an attempt to gain favor with politicians nearly fifty-five years later, what transpired is strange, bordering on unexplainable. A week later, a missive from "An Old Confederate" told a differing story:

> We had not intended ever to tell what we know of the West Florida Cadets but we believe in "giving honor where honor is due" and the brave men who defended us at Natural Bridge shall not be defrauded on the pages of history for lack of courage on our part to speak the truth. The true tale of the cadets is a pitiful one.[164]

The Old Confederate continued that upon seeing the stretcher carrying a badly injured Confederate, the boys cried and ran.

> It was a mistake to have taken these children into such a place; they trembled, they turned, their knees knocked together, some of them began to cry, and with one accord they broke ranks and ran. That had to be stopped—it might create a panic and the day be lost; so some of the other officers came to Captain Johnson's assistance, and by coaxing and forcing got them into line again, and with a guard in the rear they went forward not, however, to a very exposed position. Captain Johnson was terribly mortified and so were the cadets at first, but on their return home the little girls of Bel-Air met the train with laurel wreaths for each young hero (?) and by the time they reached Tallahassee and were welcomed by their anxious relatives they were ready to forget what had happened and believe themselves all the little girls had said they were.[165]

The response to the Old Confederate was fast and universal. Susan Archer wrote, "It is hoped that the party who wrote the scurrilous [sic] and cowardly article about our boys will be manly enough to acknowledge his mistake, under his own name, as a true Confederate would never have been guilty of writing so vile an article." Several former cadets chimed in, including one who volunteered that several former cadets were proud members of the Ku Klux Klan and had produced "splendid results—a restored south, and white supremacy."[166]

This photo, taken by Charles Schaeffer, shows the grandeur of the monument dedicated at the site of the Battle of Natural Bridge on Confederate Memorial Day, April 26, 1922. The eagle seen topping the monument was removed for conservation in 2011. *State Archives of Florida.*

The controversy seemingly vanished after several weeks with no clear indication as to the identity of the "Old Confederate." Susan Archer, however, was sure she knew their identity. A typescript of the Old Confederate article is part of the James Tillinghast Archer papers at Florida State University. The article has an annotation in Susan Archer's handwriting: "Written by Mrs. Sue Eppes. The aforesaid 'Old Confederate' hadn't courage enough to write this under her own name." The reason for Archer's belief and what Eppes's motives may have been remain vague at best. Archer's handwritten note continues: "Was brought about in after years. Caused by a case of spite or pique, which was a personal matter [and] had nothing to do with the war."[167]

After years of effort, the Anna Jackson Chapter of the United Daughters of the Confederacy received a donation of two acres of battlefield. George W. Rhode was to donate an additional four acres of battlefield land in 1921. Later that year, the Florida legislature appropriated $5,000 for the Anna Jackson Chapter to appoint a committee to oversee the erection of a monument on the property.

On April 26, 1922, Confederate Memorial Day, in front of a crowd of nearly three thousand, the monument was unveiled and dedicated. The nearly twenty-foot-tall granite monument consists of a large pedestal and base. In 2011, the Florida Park Service removed the bronze-covered eagle that originally topped the monument.

Events of the day included hymn singing, prayers and speeches by dignitaries, including Jacksonville mayor John W. Martin. Young descendants of Civil War veterans, including the grandniece of General William Miller, unveiled the grand monument. A celebratory fish fry and barbecue concluded the festivities.

In March 2000, a new, rectangular monument commemorating both Union and Confederate soldiers killed at, or because of injuries sustained at, the Battle of Natural Bridge was added to the site. Today, the State of Florida owns the park.[168]

Chapter 7

THE LINCOLN ASSASSINATION

Located far from the major events of the war and certainly far from the tragic events of the night of April 14, 1865, Florida played a role in the post–Lincoln assassination story. Florida or Floridians played no role in the assassination; rather, key figures in the assassination story were to end up in Florida.

Dr. Samuel A. Mudd Sr., the physician who performed surgery on the severely injured assassin John Wilkes Booth, spent several years confined with other assassination participants at Fort Jefferson in the Dry Tortugas, south of the Florida mainland.

Lewis Thornton Powell was hanged for his role in the Lincoln assassination. Powell has an unusual connection to the small community of Geneva. In the small Geneva Community Cemetery, the most easily visited remains of Powell are interred. Here, in 1994, the skull of Powell was buried in a plot next to that of his mother.

The stories of Powell and Mudd, while intertwined, veer apart dramatically, and they came to be associated with Florida through very different means.

LEWIS POWELL (PAINE OR PAYNE)

Lewis Thornton Powell was born on April 22, 1844, the eighth of thirteen children, to the Reverend George Cader Powell and Patience Caroline Powell. George and Patience were second cousins. Lewis's older brother

Lewis Powell (Payne) served in the Second Florida Infantry before being wounded during the Battle of Gettysburg. Powell later played a key role in the Abraham Lincoln assassination conspiracy, severely wounding Secretary of State Edwin Stanton and several others. Powell was put to death for his involvement. Today, his skull is buried in Geneva Cemetery in Florida. *Library of Congress.*

Oliver H. Powell died on January 6, 1863, most likely from infection in a wound he suffered during the Battle of Murfreesboro. A second brother, George Washington Powell, was badly injured, shot in the arm during the Petersburg campaign in September 1864. The Civil War was not kind to the Confederate-backing Powell family.[169]

Powell was born in Randolph County, Alabama, and earned the nickname "Doc" due to his love of animals. Living in the Deep South, Powell saw the slave system firsthand during his formative years. No doubt the childhood experiences he and his brothers grew up with influenced their decisions to join the Confederate army. George Powell had hopes for a career in the church for his son once the family moved to Florida. "When Lewis was twelve, he became seriously interested in religion. He helped his father on the farm, and was described as kind and tenderhearted, yet determined in all his undertakings. He was highly regarded by his friends and associates in the Live Oak area. His sisters adored him, later describing him as a 'lovable, sweet, kind young boy.'"[170]

Shortly after Florida seceded from the Union, Powell volunteered for military service, joining the Hamilton Blues, commanded by Henry J. Steward. In June 1861, the Blues became Company I of the Second Florida Infantry and were mustered into Confederate service on July 13, 1861. In rapid order, they transferred north, arriving in Virginia shortly after the Confederate victory at Manassas. Over the next few months, the Second Florida stayed in Virginia, guarding Union prisoners and going through training drills.

Historians believe that Powell first became acquainted with John Wilkes Booth during this period. While stationed near Richmond, Powell received a night pass and attended a theater performance. After the play, Powell was introduced to Booth, who had impressed the novice theatergoer considerably. They would not have much time to strike up a friendship; the Second Florida moved southeast to Yorktown, joining the Army of the Peninsula in September 1861. It was during the Siege of Yorktown in spring 1862 that the young Powell saw his first combat action. Throughout 1862, Powell and the Second Florida saw considerable action. Now serving under General Jubal Early, the Second took part in fighting at Williamsburg, Seven Pines, Gaines Mill, Frayser's Farm, Second Manassas, Harper's Ferry, Antietam and Fredericksburg.

During the summer of 1862, Powell's one-year enlistment expired. He was convinced to reenlist, receiving a fifty-dollar bounty for taking the place of S.R. Chisman. Powell would have received the news of his older brother Oliver's death in early 1863, and in May 1863, he received a furlough. It is uncertain where he went, because his father stated that he did not see him again after his 1861 enlistment.

The summer of 1863 was to prove a turning point in the war and for the Second Florida. Now a part of the Army of Northern Virginia, they joined their fellow Confederates in the march into Pennsylvania, taking part in perhaps the seminal battle of the war, the Battle of Gettysburg. It was during the ferocious July 3 fighting that Powell was shot in the right wrist and later taken prisoner. Confined to Camp Letterman in Gettysburg, Powell was later transferred to the United States Army Hospital in Baltimore, Maryland.

It was in Gettysburg, while assisting in the care of more seriously injured patients, that Powell made the acquaintance of Ms. Margaret Branson, a volunteer nurse from Baltimore. Ms. Branson returned home to Maryland and Private Powell transferred to Baltimore around the same time. On September 7, Powell escaped his confinement, visiting Ms. Branson and telling her he was going to cross the lines south into the Confederacy. This was to be her last contact with Powell until January 1865.

Powell did not rejoin the Second Florida; rather, during the latter months of 1863, he joined a cavalry regiment led by Colonel John Singleton Mosby, known as Mosby's Rangers. Powell did not stay with Mosby long. In early January 1865, he entered Alexandria, and on the thirteenth, he took the Oath of Allegiance, using the alias Lewis Payne out of concern for retaliation by Mosby's men. After taking the oath, Powell left for Baltimore. Here, in February, he encountered his old friend John Wilkes Booth. Booth had already formulated his plan to kidnap President Lincoln and ferry him south. Booth needed several strong men to assist in the deed, and in Powell, he had a prime candidate. "Here was a strong, battle-hardened, destitute, and desperate man, well-qualified in every way to carry out Booth's nefarious crime." Over the next few weeks, the friends would meet often, usually at the Barnum Hotel and the Branson house.[171]

John Wilkes Booth assigned members of the conspiracy differing tasks. Booth took the prime assignment for himself: the murder of President Abraham Lincoln. Vice President Andrew Johnson was to be assassinated by George Atzerodt. Lewis Powell, along with David Herold, was to assassinate Secretary of State William Seward, who at the time was confined to his bed after a carriage accident.[172]

The young Powell was hot of temper, and this nearly derailed his participation in Booth's plan. While still in Baltimore, Powell was involved in a physical altercation with an African American house cleaner at the Branson house. He claimed that she spoke to him in a rude manner, refused to clean his room as directed and called him by derogatory names. Powell struck the woman on her forehead, tossed her to the floor and made statements that he would kill her. Once Powell left her, she reported his actions to military authorities, who, on March 10, 1865, arrested Powell.[173]

While Powell was in custody, Lieutenant H.B. Smith interviewed him. Smith thought little of Powell's intellect, describing him as a "sullen, dumb-looking, overgrown young man; a cross between a big booby and a sullen animal." In a rambling confession, Powell wrote, "I whipped a colored woman at the house on Monday last, because she insulted me; her name is Annie." He signed the note "L. Paine."[174]

As there were no witnesses, and given the seemingly minor nature of the offense, authorities released Powell after he took the Oath of Allegiance. Concerned about Powell's loyalty, Smith required "Paine" to move north of Philadelphia and stay that far north for the duration of the war. Paine promptly departed for New York City but, by March 14, had returned to Washington, D.C., where he took up residence at the Surratt Boarding House.[175]

Powell reunited with Booth and the other conspirators on March 15 at Gautier's Saloon, where they made final plans for the kidnapping of the president. On the evening of March 17, Booth led the conspirators, including Arnold, Atzerodt, Herrold, O'Laughlin, Powell and John Surratt, in a failed kidnapping attempt. The kidnapping plan fell apart when President Lincoln did not attend a play at the Campbell Hospital as Booth anticipated. The plotters briefly reunited at the Surratt House before going their separate ways, leaving town in case they were being sought.[176]

Early in the evening of April 14, 1865, John Wilkes Booth assembled a select group from his motley crew and provided instructions. Booth gave Powell a knife, a gun and instructions to kill Secretary of State William Seward. Powell rented a horse and rode to the Seward residence. He sounded the doorbell and a servant, William Bell, answered. Powell concocted a story of having medicine for the sick Seward. Either Bell let Powell in, or Powell pushed past him and clumsily made his way upstairs, arousing Frederick William Seward, the secretary's son, in the process. Frederick denied the assassin entrance to Seward's chamber, and Powell started down the stairs as if to leave.

Powell was in no mood to leave, however. After descending only a few steps, he whirled around, pistol in hand, and went after the surprised Frederick. Powell pointed his gun directly at Frederick and pulled the trigger. There was a dull metallic *click*. For some reason, the weapon did not fire. Powell then savagely beat the younger Seward with the gun so viciously that the revolver broke, the plunger lodging between the gun's frame and cylinder, preventing the weapon from firing. The cylinder itself eventually fell out, rendering the gun useless for firing. Frederick lay on the floor bleeding profusely, with a fractured skull.[177]

Powell crashed into Secretary Seward's bedroom, attacking the already injured man and severely injuring Seward in the neck and face. A male nurse and another of Seward's sons, Augustus, attempted to subdue Powell. During the melee, Powell repeatedly yelled, "I'm mad, I'm mad." Seward's protectors, despite having been injured by the knife-wielding assassin themselves, were able to force the attacker from the bedchamber. Powell ran down the stairs, stabbing a messenger by the name of Emerick Hansell in the process.[178]

Upon reaching the street, Powell found himself alone and confused, unable to find the Navy Yard Bridge where he was to meet Booth. After three days of hiding, Powell returned to the Surratt boardinghouse in the late evening hours of April 17, where he tried to disguise himself as a

William Seward served as governor of New York and spent two terms as a United States senator from the state. Lewis Powell, as a part of the Lincoln assassination plot, attacked the staunchly antislavery secretary of state. Seward was injured severely in the attack but survived. *Library of Congress.*

laborer hired by Mrs. Surratt to dig a gutter. Unfortunately for Powell, War Department officials were at the boarding house and had Mrs. Surratt and others under arrest. Surratt denied knowing the man, and War Department officers, not believing her story, arrested Powell for further questioning.

Early in the morning of April 18, police brought William Bell, William Seward's servant, to headquarters and asked him to review a lineup of men. He identified Powell as the attacker of Secretary Seward and others in the home. Police promptly bound Powell, placed a canvas bag over his head and confined him aboard the *Saugus,* anchored in the Potomac.

In total, the government charged eight individuals in varying degrees for the assassination conspiracy, Lewis Powell (tried under the name Lewis Payne), David E. Herold, George A. Atzerodt, Michael O'Laughlin, Edman Spangler, Samuel Arnold, Mary E. Surratt, and Doctor Samuel A. Mudd. Charges against Powell included conspiring to kill President Abraham Lincoln and assault and attempt to murder Secretary of State William Seward, Frederick Seward, Augustus Seward, Emerick Hansell and George Robinson.

At the direction of President Andrew Johnson, the War Department appointed a ten-man commission to serve as jurors. The court assigned William E. Doster to defend Powell. Doster put together a long defense, ending with a summation arguing that jurors should have spared Powell's life because he was a victim. Doster claimed Powell was a victim of slavery, the horrors of war and his own imagination.[179]

The men shown in this image are members of the military commission whose job it was to determine the guilt or innocence of those accused in the Abraham Lincoln assassination conspiracy. Four conspirators were sentenced to hanging, including Mary Surratt, and three were sentenced to life in prison. *Library of Congress.*

Despite his attorney's best efforts, the commission found Powell/Payne guilty on all charges on July 6, 1865, by the minimum two-thirds majority required for the most severe punishment. His punishment: death by hanging the following day.

During the nearly two-month trial, the commission heard testimony from 371 witnesses. More than 100 witnesses did not take the stand despite receiving a subpoena. In the years since the trial, many students of the event have raised the question of whether the accused received a fair trial or if a military commission was even the correct legal procedure.[180]

On July 7, 1865, Powell, Herrold, Atzerodt and Surratt were executed at the Old Arsenal Penitentiary, now known as Fort Lesley J. McNair. Authorities allowed the bodies of the convicted assassins to hang for approximately thirty minutes before they unceremoniously cut them down, placed them in plain wooden boxes and buried them in the prison yard.[181]

In the years after the execution, the remains of the conspirators were moved several times. In 1867, they were reburied outside at Warehouse #1 on the prison grounds. Sometime around 1870, the crumbling remains of Lewis Powell were dug up, removed from the prison grounds and moved to Glenwood Cemetery. Glenwood is the final known resting place of fellow conspirator George Atzerodt, who is buried in an unmarked grave. The undertaker in charge of this move was Joseph Gawler. In 1884, Powell's remains were again exhumed and reinterred. The final resting place for the

This powerful image taken by Alexander Gardner shows the hooded figures of Mary Surratt, Lewis Powell/Payne, David Herold and George Atzerodt moments before they were put to death for their role in the assassination of Abraham Lincoln. *Library of Congress.*

majority of his remains is at Rock Creek Cemetery in Washington, D.C., though he is not recognized in their extensive listing of notable burials. His remains are believed to be located in section K, lots 21, 22 and 23, a section noted as "Unknown—removed from Holmead." Again, Joseph Gawler is listed as the undertaker in charge of the reinterment.[182]

Experts believe that during 1870 or 1884, Gawler removed Powell's skull and provided it to the Army Medical Museum, then located in Ford's Theater. The skull was identified as item 2244, the "skull of a white male."[183] In 1898, skull 2244 and the remains of many Native Americans were transferred to the care of the Smithsonian Institution, where they remained stored for nearly one hundred years. In 1990, Congress passed the Native American Graves Protection and Repatriation Act. This law directed and "provided for the repatriation and disposition of certain Native American human remains, funerary objects, sacred objects, and objects of cultural patrimony." In complying with this act, the Smithsonian began reviewing their collections, and in 1991, anthropologist Stuart Speaker discovered Powell's skull mingled with a collection of Native bones.[184]

At the time of the Lincoln assassination, Lewis Powell's family was living in Live Oak, Florida, a small community in the north central part of Florida. During the Civil War, Live Oak and the surrounding region were a critical railroad area as the Confederacy tried to move goods from the state northward to fighting armies.

During the trial of Powell and the other conspirators, Powell's attorney, William Doster, attempted to contact George Powell, the father of the accused. Doster received no reply until October, months after Powell's execution. George, in his letter, explained he had been ill and not able to travel. When he was finally well and able to make the train trip to Washington, it was too late. Upon arriving in Jacksonville, he heard the news of the execution and thus returned home.

The *Florida Union* newspaper out of Jacksonville reported on George's visit to the city. The report explained the toll the recent war had taken upon the Powell family. George had lost a son fighting, another son was maimed and finally, there were Lewis's actions and his execution. While the newspaper expressed sympathy for George Powell, they did believe Lewis Powell's punishment was just.[185]

Shortly after word of Lewis's execution, the Powell family left Live Oak, moving south to Orange County. Historian Leon O. Prior writes that a mixture of grief, humiliation and George's missionary zeal caused the move. The family settled near Lake Jessup, near Sanford and Geneva. George's burial location is unknown. Lewis Powell's mother, Caroline Patience Powell, is buried in Geneva Cemetery.[186]

The story of Lewis Thornton Powell did not end with the discovery of his skull in a Smithsonian collection, however. Now, knowing the infamous nature of the mystery skull, Lincoln assassination expert Michael Kaufman set about finding the Powell's closest descendent and began the process of convincing Smithsonian leadership to relinquish the skull to that relative.

As might be expected, multiple potential relatives laid claim to the remains. In the spring of 1993, the Smithsonian made the determination that a woman claiming Powell impregnated her great-grandmother during the time he was associating with Booth at the Surratt boardinghouse was the closest living descendent. The woman's unnamed ancestor had mysteriously vanished to Canada, where she allegedly gave birth to her and Powell's child. The unnamed descendent wished for the Powell skull to stay with the Smithsonian, a choice that raised eyebrows of those watching events unfold.[187]

Lincoln assassination experts were quick to raise questions about the authenticity of this claim, pointing out there was no evidence that Powell fathered a child. These historians do not discount that Powell had friendships, perhaps intimate ones, with at least two known women—a woman in Baltimore named Mary Branson and another in Virginia, Betty Meredith—during his time with Mosby's Rangers.[188]

Less than two years later, however, the Smithsonian had reexamined the case and determined that Lewis Powell was the great-uncle of Geneva resident Helen Alderman and that she was the closest descendent. On Saturday, November 12, 1994, under a warm sun, with the Reverend Daryl Permenter Sr., pastor of the First Baptist Church of Oviedo, officiating, the skull of Lewis Thornton Powell, now contained in a small mahogany box, was buried in a permanent location, near the remains of his mother in Geneva Cemetery. Ms. Alderman stated, "It's a closing for the family. This has been hanging over the family for a long time."[189]

Geneva Cemetery is open to the public. Visitors may tour the grounds, viewing hundreds of burials, including the final resting place of Lincoln conspirator Lewis Powell and sixteen other Civil War soldiers, both Union and Confederate.[190]

Samuel Mudd

The role of Dr. Samuel Mudd was clearly different from that played by Lewis Powell. While not a murderer, he was a crucial part of the conspiracy, and his actions could have led to the escape of John Wilkes Booth. For his participation in the conspiracy, the military commission convicted and sentenced Mudd to life in prison.

The descendants of Samuel Mudd have made multiple efforts to have his name cleared. These efforts have hinged on two primary arguments. The first: Mudd was innocent, a doctor who assisted an injured man in keeping with his calling. The second argument stems from the legality of the military commission and its place in passing judgment on civilians.[191]

While Mudd did not have a direct hand in the murder and attempted murders on the evening of April 14, 1865, he is known to have associated with John Wilkes Booth multiple times in the lead-up to the murder. During Mudd's trial, it came out that he and Booth had met on more than one occasion prior to the morning that Booth and David Herrold appearing on the doctor's doorstep seeking medical attention.

Mudd had admitted to the government in writing that he met with Booth in November 1864: "I have seen J. Wilkes Booth. I was introduced to him by Mr. J.C. Thompson, a son-in-law of Dr. William Queen, in November or December last." He did not, however, prove forthcoming about a second meeting that took place in December 1864. He claimed to investigator Colonel H.H. Wells: "I have never seen Booth since that time to my knowledge until last Saturday night (April 15)."[192]

According to testimony provided by Samuel Mudd, about four in the morning on April 15, a pounding at their front door awakened the doctor and his wife. Mudd answered, finding two men, one on horseback and the other holding the reins. Mudd saw the rider was in need of medical attention and invited them inside. He assisted the injured man upstairs, put him in a bed and began treatment. Mudd cut the boot from the injured man's leg and determined that the leg was in fact broken, approximately two inches above the ankle joint. He set the bones and created a splint to keep them in place.

Doctor Samuel A. Mudd was convicted of aiding and conspiring in the assassination of President Abraham Lincoln. Mudd's life was spared by a single vote. He received a sentence of life in prison but served less than four years, receiving a pardon from President Andrew Johnson after his actions during a yellow fever outbreak at Fort Jefferson. *State Archives of Florida.*

After this impromptu surgery, Mudd had breakfast with the uninjured traveler, the man we know to be David E. Herold. Herold told Mudd that his name was Henson and that Booth's name was Tyser or Tyson; Mudd was unsure. After breakfast, Herold requested a razor that his companion could use. When the noon meal was complete Mudd noticed that Booth had shaved his mustache but retained his beard.

Later that afternoon, Mudd and Herold rode to the home of Henry Lowe Mudd Sr., Samuel's father, in an attempt to buy a carriage to transport the injured Booth. They found neither the elder Mudd nor a carriage. From here, they proceeded toward Bryantown, with Herold considerably in front of Mudd. Nearing Bryantown, however, Herold wheeled his horse around and headed back toward Mudd, proclaiming, "I believe I will get my friend to go to Rev. Wilmer's on horseback."[193]

Mudd testified that he continued on to Bryantown, making several purchases before hearing the news of the Lincoln assassination. On his return home, he stopped at the home of a neighbor, Francis Farrell, where he told Farrell the news of the president's death and the attack at the Seward home. Farrell later testified that Mudd told him a man by the name of Booth was to blame for the attacks.

Upon arriving home, Mudd found his houseguests mounted on their horses, preparing to leave. Herold asked Mudd for directions to the home of Parson Wilmer. Mudd provided directions taking the men through Zekiah Swamp.

The following morning, Sunday, April 16, Samuel Mudd attended worship services and met with his cousin George Mudd. According to testimony from George, Samuel admitted to the visit from two suspicious people. George recommended reporting this visit, but Samuel demurred, asking George to do it for him.

The following morning, nearly two days after Booth and Herold left the Samuel Mudd home, George reported the events to Lieutenant Dana, a member of the Thirteenth New York Volunteer Cavalry. Nobody—except for Samuel Mudd, perhaps—was aware that John Wilkes Booth was attempting to escape on a broken leg. Based on George Mudd's report, government authorities visited and questioned Samuel on April 18, April 21 and April 22. It was based on these inquiries that Samuel created what is known as the "voluntary statement" and Colonel H.H. Wells drafted the "Wells statement."[194]

Authorities deemed it critical to search the Mudd house for evidence during the questioning on April 21, when Samuel asked his wife to go upstairs and retrieve the boot he cut from the man's leg. Mudd had neglected to tell investigators he had this evidence, again raising their suspicions of his complicity. Investigator Lieutenant Lovett discovered the name J. Wilkes along the upper edge of the boot. Mudd claimed not to have seen this crucial detail. Lovett took Mudd into custody and delivered him to Colonel H.H. Wells in Bryantown.

During the trip to Bryantown, Mudd became somewhat more forthcoming. He admitted that he met Booth in late 1864 and that the man authorities now wanted for assassinating the president of the United States had stayed at his home as a guest. Upon seeing a photo of Booth and being asked if this was the man with the broken leg, Mudd hedged his bets, stating that it did resemble him "across the eyes."

Mudd returned to Bryantown for further questioning on April 22. It was on this date he signed the "Wells statement." Assured of Mudd's complicity, Wells had the doctor taken into custody on April 24 and then transported to Washington, D.C., where investigators held him at the Capitol Prison.

The government laid out the case against Samuel A. Mudd in the charges against him:

> *The said Samuel A. Mudd did…advise, encourage, receive, entertain, harbor and conceal, aid and assist, the said John Wilkes Booth…with knowledge of the murderous and traitorous conspiracy aforesaid, and with intent to aid, abet, and assist…in the execution thereof, and in escaping justice after the murder of the said Abraham Lincoln.*[195]

Historian Edward Steers Jr. concisely states the government claims as: "1) participating in the plot to assassinate Lincoln, and 2) knowingly aiding and abetting the escape of Lincoln's murder." Steers states that Mudd did not know about the murder plot; rather, the murder was an extension of the kidnapping plot, which Mudd did know about.[196]

During the trial of Samuel Mudd, evidence was shown proving that the doctor was untruthful to government investigators on several occasions and that his claims of only having met Booth a single time were false. With War Department–appointed jurors strongly stacked against him, Mudd was found guilty. A five to four vote spared his life and sent him to life in prison rather than the gallows. He was confined to Fort Jefferson, located in the Dry Tortugas, seventy miles west of Key West. Fort Jefferson would be his home for almost four years, a home he would share with fellow conspirators Michael O'Laughlen, Samuel Arnold and Edman Spangler.[197]

Fort Jefferson was authorized in 1845 under President James K. Polk to guard and protect the Gulf Coast of the United States. Construction of the fort on Garden Key was begun in 1847 using slave labor, northern carpenters and prison labor. The project was beset with an assortment of roadblocks, including lack of funds and materials; poor weather, including hurricanes; and sickness, notably yellow fever. The fort was abandoned in 1874; work was never completed. The United States Navy received control of the location in 1882 and used the fort as a coal supply base for its Caribbean operations. Fort Jefferson received national monument status in 1935. Today, visitors can tour the premises, accessing the property by ferry, seaplane or private boat. For the more adventurous, camping is allowed on Garden Key for a nominal fee.[198]

Life in prison at Fort Jefferson was never meant to be easy—and it was not. Those confined there dealt with harsh living conditions. The food was often rotting, and sickness was common among prisoners and guards. Common ailments included dysentery, scurvy and diarrhea. Writing to his wife, Mudd

This aerial view of Fort Jefferson shows the isolation that prisoners and Union troops stationed here during the Civil War would have experienced. Residents of the fort were seventy miles from Key West. *Library of Congress.*

described his confinement: "I am nearly worn out, the weather is almost suffocating, and millions of mosquitos, fleas, and bedbugs infest the whole island. We can't rest day or night in peace for the mosquitos."[199]

Shortly after his confinement, Dr. Mudd made the decision to try to escape. The plan became cemented in his mind due not only to poor conditions but also a planned change of military personnel. When the conspirators arrived, the 110th and 161st New York Infantry were stationed at the fort. In September 1865, however, the 82nd United States Colored Troops arrived. Mudd was an ardent secessionist and a former slave owner. He was unable to accept such a fate and had considerable concerns for his own safety.

While escape seems like a difficult proposition, since the fort was isolated far from land, it was not an uncommon occurrence. Upon Mudd's arrival, authorities assigned him to the fort's hospital, where he was able to use his skills and enjoyed a slightly higher standard of living than run-of-the-mill inmates. In his medical role, Mudd received more casual treatment from his jailers. He was able to witness nearly forty other prisoners make successful escapes, usually aboard supply ships returning to the mainland. Mudd was careful, though. Knowing his mail was monitored, he even wrote to his wife, "I have had several opportunities to make my escape, but knowing, or believing, it would show guilt, I have resolved to remain peaceable and quiet, and allow the Government the full exercise of its power, justice, and clemency. Should I take French leave, it would amount to expatriation, which I don't feel disposed to do at present."[200] He would not remain peaceable and quiet for long.

The supply ship *Thomas A. Scott* arrived at Fort Jefferson on September 25, 1865. Knowing that security was slight, Mudd changed into a suit of clothes and boarded the ship, where Henry Kelly, a young seaman whose introduction to the conspirator is still shrouded in mystery, met him. Kelly helped hide Mudd below deck underneath some loose floorboards. When it came time for the ship to depart, guards undertook a standard prisoner check, noting that the prominent prisoner Samuel Mudd was missing. A search of the ship turned up the missing doctor, who was quick to point a finger at young Henry Kelly for his assistance.

For his troubles, Mudd was relieved of medical duties and placed under close watch. Mudd recalled,

> *I was put in the guard house, with chains on hands and feet, and closely confined for two days. An order then came from the Major for me to be put to hard labor, wheeling sand. I was placed under a boss, who put me to cleaning old bricks. I worked hard all day, and came very near finishing one brick. The order also directs the Provost Marshal to have me closely confined on the arrival of every steamer until she departs.*[201]

Mudd did not hold back in letters home as to the reason for his escape attempt. He wrote to his wife, "It is bad enough to be a prisoner in the hands of white men, your equals under the Constitution, but to be lorded over by a set of ignorant, prejudiced, and irresponsible beings of the unbleached humanity was more than I could submit to when I had every reason to believe my chances of escape almost certain, and would be crowned with success." He also wrote to his brother-in-law Jeremiah Dyer of "the humiliation of being guarded by an ignorant, irresponsible & prejudiced negro Soldiery, before an Enlightened People as a justification. We are now guarded entirely by negro soldiers & a few white Officers a skins difference."[202]

Perhaps accepting his fate, or due to increased scrutiny and security, Mudd was never to try to escape again. The same cannot be said for Henry Kelly, the seaman who helped Mudd attempt his escape. Kelly was confined to the dungeon with another prisoner by the last name of Smith. According to lore, the men escaped their shackles and lowered themselves out of a broken window. They robbed a civilian merchant of clothing, food and a small amount of cash before stealing a boat and leaving the island.[203]

The weather and mosquito problem led to a crisis in August 1867. By August 21, at least four cases of yellow fever had hit the island fortress. At the time, scientists believed the cause of yellow fever to be bad air that led to high fever, "black vomit" and jaundice, the basis for the name yellow fever. Medical science did not understand the viral nature of yellow fever and the role of mosquitos in transmitting it.[204]

Despite a decline in the number of prisoners on the island, there were a considerable number of troops still stationed there—more than four hundred people in total. Cases spread rapidly, with one company of soldiers reporting thirty new cases in a single day. The virus did not spare the Lincoln conspirators. On September 17, Arnold and O'Laughlen contracted the disease. Arnold survived; O'Laughlen did not. Samuel Mudd and Edman Spangler escaped the ravages of yellow fever.

After the death of Joseph Smith, the post physician, on September 8, Mudd bravely volunteered to take charge at the Fort Jefferson hospital. There was no agreement for a pardon in this effort. Despite not having a clear understanding of how a person contracted yellow fever, Mudd attempted to implement procedures to help lessen patients' struggles. Mudd ended the policy of quarantine, correctly believing that this did nothing to prevent the spread of disease. As did most doctors of the day, Mudd believed it best to encourage sweating when treating a fever. He did this using calomel to induce vomiting and Dover's powder, which contained ipecac and opium and produced heavy sweating. Mudd required clean bedding and clothing for patients.

Under the guidance of Dr. Mudd, fatality rates remained surprisingly low. Mudd treated 270 cases, of which 38 were to die, a fatality rate of 14 percent. In comparison, an 1873 outbreak at Fort Jefferson led to 37 infections and 14 deaths, or a fatality rate of almost 37 percent. While not a miracle worker, Dr. Samuel Mudd had lessened the suffering of many victims and saved numerous lives, all while putting himself in peril.[205]

Dr. Mudd's efforts did not go unnoticed or unappreciated. Many of those at Fort Jefferson believed that Mudd deserved clemency for his actions. Lieutenant Edmund L. Zalinski petitioned President Andrew Johnson on Mudd's behalf. In part, he wrote, "[Mudd] inspired the hopeless with courage, and by his constant presence in the midst of danger and infection, regardless of his own life, tranquillized the fearful and desponding. Many here who have experienced his kind and judicious treatment can never repay him."[206] Almost three hundred men signed this notice, both officers and enlisted men.[207]

There can be little doubt that this was a difficult decision for Johnson. Abraham Lincoln was the beloved, martyred president who brought the country together in many people's minds. True, there was not universal love for Lincoln, but his memory stood strong. Mudd, while more involved in the conspiracy than he would admit, had not been involved in a murder plot. When times grew desperate, he helped his fellow men, even though many were Union men.

On February 8, 1869, President Andrew Johnson signed the hoped-for pardon, stating in part,

> *Samuel A. Mudd devoted himself to the care and cure of the sick, and interposed his courage and his skill to protect the garrison, otherwise without medical aid, from peril and alarm, and thus, as the officers and men unite in testifying, saved many valuable lives and earned the admiration and the gratitude of all who observed or experienced his generous and faithful service to humanity.*[208]

The government released Mudd from prison on March 8, 1869. He had served nearly four years of his original life sentence. Mudd arrived home in Maryland on March 20. He returned to the practice of medicine and cultivated tobacco. The Mudd family grew, eventually including nine children in total, though only seven would outlive Samuel. On January 10, 1883, Samuel Mudd died from what historians believe was pneumonia, leaving a complicated legacy that his heirs have battled with for more than a century.[209]

Today, the legacy of Samuel A. Mudd is still visible at Fort Jefferson, in a room at the far end of the south bastion in what is called Dr. Mudd's Cell. The room includes a photo of Mudd and a plaque containing a quotation from the pardon granted by President Johnson. There is only slight evidence that Mudd was ever imprisoned in this exact room. It does serve, however, as a permanent reminder of how Fort Jefferson played a role in the lives of several men associated with the Lincoln assassination conspiracy.[210]

Chapter 8

VISITING THE CIVIL WAR IN FLORIDA

P art of the joy of studying the American Civil War is the possibility of visiting many of the locations associated with it. As we know, Florida was not a major fighting area, with only one true battle occurring in the state, along with several larger skirmishes. When it comes to monuments and markers, it is important to remember that many communities have removed Confederate iconography from public spaces. This makes printed references like Lees and Gaske's book, *Recalling Deeds Immortal: Florida Monuments to the Civil War*, outdated as travel guides but still important in historical study. There are many locations, however, that the student of the Civil War should consider seeking out, some of which are listed below. For more, students of the Civil War should seek to obtain a copy of Frederick Gaske's valuable booklet *Florida Civil War Heritage Trail*.[211]

Listed in this chapter are a few gems I recommend you visit. Some are, of course, more accessible than others are. All, however, are worthy of your consideration.

OLUSTEE BATTLEFIELD HISTORIC STATE PARK

5815 Battlefield Trail Road
Olustee, FL 32087
https://www.floridastateparks.org/parks-and-trails/
olustee-battlefield-historic-state-park

For students of the Civil War in Florida, the Battle of Olustee is the "big one." While I have avoided discussion of this battle, that is not out of disrespect for it. Rather, I would refer the reader to one of several full-length books that provide detailed description of the days surrounding the battle.[212]

It was on February 20, 1864, that more than ten thousand Union and Confederate troops did battle. Union troops, including a large number of United States Colored Troops (USCT) under the command of Brigadier General Truman Seymour, were driving west from Jacksonville with the goal of interrupting supply shipments bound for Confederate forces fighting further north. They met Confederate forces under the command of Brigadier General Joseph Finegan. Union forces had a slight numerical edge over their Confederate foes.

The outcome of the battle was decisive for the Confederates, however. Union forces were driven east toward Jacksonville. The battle was bloody for both sides. Union casualties were over 1,800, with more than 200 dead. Confederate forces suffered approximately 950 casualties, with 93 dead. In addition to preventing Union damage to supply lines, the Confederate victory ended Northern hopes of returning Florida to the Union.

Today, visitors can view a portion of the battlefield by taking a mile-long trail that includes interpretive panels to help guide readers through the action of the day. Also on site are several monuments commemorating those who did battle.

The monument that is most prominent has a racially tinged past. When the Florida legislature, in 1899, originally allocated $2,500 to erect a monument at Olustee, they stated that it was to be for "the Federal and Confederate officers and soldiers who participated in said battle." The United Daughters of the Confederacy (UDC), who were the main backers of this monument, decried this, stating that "they did not care to divide honors intended for the Confederate dead with negro dead of the Union army." When the legislature reconvened in 1901, the UDC's demands were granted: the monument was to be only for Confederate officers and soldiers.[213]

Left: Truman Seymour began the war commanding a company of artillery against Confederate attack at Fort Sumter. In 1864, Seymour was placed in charge of the Division of Florida and led his troops west from Jacksonville on a raid that ended in failure at the Battle of Olustee. *Library of Congress.*

Right: Confederate troops led by Brigadier General Joseph Finegan repelled Union forces led by Union brigadier general Truman Seymour at the Battle of Olustee. After the battle, Finegan was tapped to command the Florida Brigade in the Army of Northern Virginia. *Library of Congress.*

It proved difficult to raise the additional funds needed. In 1906, the UDC issued an "urgent appeal" in order to move the project forward. In 1909, battlefield landowners Austin B. Fletcher and John and Eliza Brown donated three acres to the state. It was determined that the monument, when erected, would be placed there.

Finally, on October 23, 1912, more than a decade after the legislature backed its creation, the large granite monument, carved to resemble a castle, was unveiled. Evander Law, former Confederate major general and chair of the Olustee Monument Commission, led the ceremony. Governor Albert W. Gilchrist was on hand to accept the donation to the state.[214]

Each year, at the end of February, the largest Civil War reenactment in Florida occurs at the park. The event is well attended, with a battle reenactment, sutlers, authentic camping for participants, period medical demonstrations and more. While the state park normally has free entrance, there is a charge to enter this event.

NATURAL BRIDGE BATTLEFIELD HISTORIC STATE PARK

7502 Natural Bridge Road
Tallahassee, FL 32305
https://www.floridastateparks.org/parks-and-trails/natural-bridge-battlefield-historic-state-park

Natural Bridge has earned its name, as it is the location where the St. Marks River flows underground into a sinkhole, before reemerging above ground a quarter of a mile later.

Due to Confederate efforts and a lack of strong attempts on the part of Union troops, Tallahassee was the only state capital east of the Mississippi River to remain in Confederate hands throughout the war. During March 1865, Union troops, including members of the United States Colored Troops under command of Brigadier General John Newton, attempted to execute a plan to land troops at the St. Marks Lighthouse. Others were to sail up the St. Marks River to attack Fort Ward.

Troops led by Confederate brigadier general William Miller, met the Union forces at the lighthouse. Confederate troops were able to hold off the Union advance. Newton marched his men several miles north to the Natural Bridge site, where he was again met by an assortment of Confederate troops, including boys from the West Florida Seminary.

Having failed at both locations, Newton ordered his troops back to the Gulf shore, where he found that naval forces had failed in their mission to ascend the St. Marks River. Union casualties amounted to approximately 150, with twenty-one men dead. Confederate forces suffered fewer than thirty casualties and only three deaths.

Visitors to the park can use picnic and fishing facilities. There is an impressive marker commemorating Confederate soldiers who fought at the site. Each year, in March, there is a battle reenactment. Ranger-guided tours of the park can be arranged with a minimum of two weeks' notice. There is a nominal entry fee to the park.

BARRANCAS NATIONAL CEMETERY

Pensacola Naval Air Station
80 Hovey Road
Pensacola, FL 32501
https://www.cem.va.gov/cems/nchp/barrancas.asp

Barrancas National Cemetery is located within the nearly twelve thousand acres of Pensacola Naval Air Station. Sections one through twelve contain the remains of more than 1,300 Civil War soldiers, both Union and Confederate.

Other burials include soldiers who perished during the Second Seminole War, World War II, Vietnam and more. Rosamond Johnson Jr., the first African American from Escambia County to die during the Korean War, is buried here. A portion of Gulf Islands National Seashore is named after Johnson. Four Medal of Honor recipients are buried in the cemetery.[215]

ST. LUKE'S CEMETERY

4362 East Lafayette Street
Marianna, FL 32446
https://www.stlukesmarianna.org/content.cfm?id=315

On September 27, 1864, a skirmish took place between roughly five hundred Union soldiers and approximately two hundred Confederate forces, made up of a mixture of home guard and Confederate regular troops. The far outnumbered Confederates were driven back to the vicinity of St. Luke's Episcopal Church. St. Luke's and several other structures were burned to the ground. Lore states that Major Nathan Cutler of the Second Maine Cavalry saved the pulpit Bible from the flames. This Bible now holds a place of honor in the rebuilt church.

Buried in the cemetery are the remains of forty Confederates, including Florida governor John Milton, district court judge George S. Hawkins and surgeon Dr. Julius T. Holden.[216]

FLORIDA HISTORIC CAPITOL

400 S. Monroe Street
Tallahassee, FL 32399
http://www.flhistoriccapitol.gov/

The Florida Secession Convention convened in this building on January 10, 1861. It was not until May 20, 1865, that Union troops were able to raise the United States flag over the building.

When crews completed construction of the new Florida capitol building in the late 1970s, the original capitol was threatened with demolition. After a successful preservation effort, this historic building was restored to its 1902 appearance and reopened in 1982. Visitors may now visit the historic capitol in person or take their choice of several interactive virtual tours.

OLD CITY CEMETERY

Martin Luther King Jr. Boulevard
between Call Street and Park Avenue
Tallahassee, FL 32301
https://www.talgov.com/realestate/res-coc-oldcity.aspx

Old City Cemetery is the oldest burying ground in Tallahassee, dating to 1821. The City of Tallahassee acquired the cemetery in 1840. Southern Whites were buried in the eastern portion of the cemetery, segregated from African Americans and Union soldiers, who received burial in the western plots. A six-foot-wide pathway, still visible today, denotes the original segregation line.

Nearly two hundred Confederate dead are buried in the cemetery. Perhaps the most recognizable name is that of Colonel David Lang. Lang commanded the Florida Brigade

A graduate of the Georgia Military Academy, Colonel David Lang commanded the Florida Brigade in the Army of Northern Virginia at the Battle of Gettysburg and was again in command at the surrender at Appomattox Court House. *State Archives of Florida.*

at both the Battle of Gettysburg and the surrender at Appomattox.[217] Just under one hundred Union troops are known to be buried in the cemetery, among them Major Edmund C. Weeks, the commander of the Second Florida Union Cavalry.

MANDARIN MUSEUM

11964 Mandarin Road
Jacksonville, FL 32223
https://www.mandarinmuseum.net/

"The wreck of the *Maple Leaf* is unsurpassed as a source for Civil War material culture. The site combines one of the largest ships sunk during the war, carrying all the possessions of more than a thousand soldiers, with a river bottom environment that perfectly preserved the ship and cargo. It is the most important repository of Civil War artifacts ever found and probably will remain so." When none other than Ed Bearss, former chief historian of the National Park Service, considered by many to have been the dean of Civil War studies, makes such a statement, it is important to listen.

This drawing by artist Alfred Waud shows the *Wreck of the Transport Steamers* Maple Leaf *and* Gen'l Hunter, in the St. Johns River. The *Maple Leaf* struck a Confederate torpedo before sinking, taking four men to their death. *Library of Congress.*

The *Maple Leaf* was a sidewheel steamboat that, in April 1864, was floating down the St. Johns River at the village of Mandarin, the City of Jacksonville less than fifteen miles ahead to the north. In the predawn hours, river pilot Romeo Murray had no way to see Confederate naval troops had mined the river. When the *Maple Leaf* struck a mine, the steamboat sank quickly. The death toll was slight; only four crewmembers perished. Murray and several of the crew returned the next day to retrieve any items they could locate. During the 1980s, Dr. Keith Holland and partners were able to locate the remains of the *Maple Leaf* and proceeded with salvage operations.

Today, the Mandarin Museum features a scale replica of the steamboat, video of salvage operations and several artifacts recovered from the site.[218]

OLD CITY CEMETERY

East Union Street between Washington and Cemetery Streets
Jacksonville, FL 32223

Old City Cemetery contains the remains of approximately 225 Confederates. Names that visitors might recognize include Brigadier General Joseph Finegan, who commanded Confederate troops at the Battle of Olustee and later served in the Army of Northern Virginia, commanding the Florida Brigade. Also interred in the cemetery is Captain Francis P. Fleming, who commanded a company at Natural Bridge. He was later to serve four years as the fifteenth governor of Florida.

Also in the cemetery is a plot dedicated to Confederates who lived in the Old Confederate Soldiers and Sailors Home that was located in Jacksonville. This home provided lodging for aged and disabled Confederate veterans. The home was in service from 1893 until 1938. Financing for the home was always difficult, and it depended on state support, in addition to donation from groups such as the United Daughters of the Confederacy. The building is no longer in existence.[219]

FORT CLINCH STATE PARK

2601 Atlantic Avenue
Fernandina Beach, FL 32034
https://www.floridastateparks.org/fortclinch

Fort Clinch, located on Amelia Island, was designed to provide protection to the port at Fernandina. Construction began in 1847, and the fort was named after General Duncan L. Clinch, who won fame for his role in the Seminole Wars. In 1861, Florida militia seized the fort from a lone keeper and two laborers. The occupation was short-lived, however, as General Robert E. Lee ordered the troops evacuated in February 1862. Union brigadier general Horatio G. Wright wrote of the Union reoccupation of the fort:

> *General: I have the honor to inform you that the combined navy and army expedition is in possession of Fernandina and the military defenses on Amelia Island, and also the batteries on the south end of Cumberland Island.*
>
> *Our occupation was a bloodless one, the rebels having evacuated on the first suspicion of our approach all the strong defenses on which they had lavished so much time and labor, removing, so far as time permitted, guns, stores, and troops. They, however, left behind no less than fourteen guns, all of large caliber.*
>
> *The town is nearly deserted of inhabitants, many of whom left reluctantly, in obedience to the orders of the rebel authorities.*[220]

The State of Florida acquired the fort in 1935, after it was deemed surplus property. The fort received considerable care under the New Deal Civilian Conservation Corps, who helped restore deteriorating portions of the fort, constructed park roads and more. Today, the fort stands as a part of the larger 1,400-acre Fort Clinch State Park. For a nominal fee, visitors can tour the fort, see a large collection of artillery and, on select weekends, witness a cannon-firing demonstration.

General Horatio G. Wright served in several capacities during the Civil War. By the end of the war, he was in charge of the Sixth Corps, following the death of John Sedgewick. After the Union occupation of Fort Clinch in 1862, Wright had the privilege to inform superior officers of the news. *Library of Congress.*

OLD PUBLIC/SLAVE MARKET

Plaza de la Constitucion
Corner of St. George and Cathedral Place near the Bridge of Lions
St. Augustine, FL 32084

Tram drivers looking to make the best story for their riders often refer to the market located in the Plaza as the Old Slave Market or similar names. This is not to say that St. Augustine did not participate in the slave trade. When we think of slave markets, images of New Orleans or Charleston often come to mind. There is no conclusive proof to show that St. Augustine ever operated anything on this level. Rather, the slave market story appears to have come from stories put forth by the likes of nineteenth-century writers Max Bloomfield and Lady Mary Anne Duffus Hardy. It was most widely spread, however, through a postcard created by local photographer W.J. Harris. This card featured an image of an elderly African American man leaning on a cane while carrying a basket over his right arm. The back of the card read "OLD SLAVE

Old Slave Market, St. Augustine, Florida.

The slave market story of St. Augustine appears to have originated from a caption on the back of a postcard similar to this. Slavery was known in the city, but the market area does not appear to have regularly functioned as a slave market in the way we think of the term. The structure in this image dates to 1888, after a fire destroyed the area in April 1887. *State Archives of Florida.*

MARKET ST. AUGUSTINE, FLA. The Old Slave Market in the east end of the Plaza is an interesting landmark of antebellum days. Old slave in foreground." Whether this was true or not, tourists mailed the image home to locations across the country, and the story became one that's repeated to this day.[222]

GREENWOOD CEMETERY

1603 Greenwood Street
Orlando, FL 32801
*https://www.orlando.gov/Our-Government/Departments-Offices/
Executive-Offices/City-Clerk/Greenwood-Cemetery*

Greenwood Cemetery was originally established in 1880, and the City of Orlando purchased it in 1892. The cemetery is now the final resting place of more than thirty-one thousand remains, including those of more than one hundred Union and one hundred Confederate soldiers.

Confederates of local significance buried at Greenwood include William H. Jewell, who served on the staff of Lieutenant General Wade Hampton and later as a Florida legislator and mayor of Orlando. James B. Parramore and John Letcher Bryan are two Confederates, also buried in Greenwood, who both later went on to serve as mayor of Orlando. James B. Parramore founded the Parramore neighborhood in the 1880s as an area specifically for those of African descent.[223]

An important Civil War addition to Greenwood Cemetery is a 1911 "Johnny Reb" statue. The United Daughters of the Confederacy originally dedicated the marble marker to statesmen, soldiers and sailors who fought for the Confederate cause. Greenwood Cemetery is now the third location for this statue. It was originally placed at the intersection of Central Boulevard and Magnolia Avenue before being moved to Lake Eola in 1917. In 2017, the statue was removed from the public park in response to concerns from local citizens.

Geneva Cemetery

240 First Street
Geneva, FL 32732
http://www.usgennet.org/usa/fl/county/seminole/Geneva/Cemteries.htm

Seventeen soldiers who served in the Civil War are buried in Geneva Cemetery. Sixteen of these are Confederates. The only known Union burial is that of Private Alexander Niblo, Company C, 104th Ohio Infantry. The most infamous burial here is that of the skull of Lewis Thornton Powell, one of the conspirators convicted in the Abraham Lincoln assassination plot.

Old Fort Park and Old Stone Wharf

Riverside Drive off Canal Street
New Smyrna Beach, FL 32168

In what is truly a great misnomer, Old Fort Park is the location of a large coquina ruins. These ruins, measuring approximately forty by eighty feet, are easily visited and can be walked on today. For many, the urge to equate these ruins to those of an early Spanish fort is too great. There is no evidence to support this claim, however. Archaeologists and historians today believe that these ruins are those of a foundation house Dr. Andrew Turnbull was building for one of his financial backers, Sir William Duncan, during the 1770s.[224]

On the location of these ruins, Jane and John Sheldon built a large wooden hotel. In 1863, the Union navy bombarded the small village, destroying the hotel. The Sheldon family built a smaller hotel after the war that stood until 1896, when it was demolished.

Just south of Old Fort Park, also on Riverside Drive, are the deteriorating remains of a Turnbull-era wharf. Nearby, Confederate soldiers from the Third Florida Infantry attacked sailors from the *Penguin* and *Henry Andrew*. Union casualties were eight dead, including two officers; several wounded; and three taken prisoner. An escaped slave guide who participated was captured and hanged. Today, a slab of coquina with a bronze plaque attached marks the site. Visitors may see the stone wharf ruins at low tide.

GAMBLE PLANTATION HISTORIC STATE PARK

3708 Patten Avenue
Ellenton, FL 34222
https://www.floridastateparks.org/parks-and-trails/judah-p-benjamin-confederate-memorial-gamble-plantation-historic-state-park

Constructed between 1845 and 1856 for sugar magnate Major Robert Gamble, the 3,500-acre plantation was sold in 1858, and in 1862, the Confederate government seized the property. In 1864, Union troops destroyed the sugar mill but did not burn the mansion. When it was under Confederate ownership, Captain Archibald McNeill served as caretaker. Archibald assisted Confederate secretary of state Judah P. Benjamin during his May 1865 escape from Florida. Secretary Benjamin stayed on the property before escaping the state by boat.

In the postwar years, the property fell into disrepair, before the United Daughters of the Confederacy purchased it in 1925. The UDC donated the home and sixteen acres to the state in 1926, retaining management of the property until 1949. In 2002, the State of Florida purchased an additional twenty acres of the original plantation. These newly acquired acres included the sugar mill ruins.

Today, visitors may tour the only surviving plantation house in South Florida. The home is furnished as that of a successful nineteenth-century plantation. The home received listing on the National Register of Historic Places in 1970.[225] While admission to the park is free, there is a small charge for house tours.

Judah P. Benjamin was elected a U.S. senator from the state of Louisiana before holding three different cabinet positions in the Jefferson Davis administration: attorney general, secretary of war, and secretary of state. After the Civil War, he escaped through Florida, spending time at the Gamble Plantation before leaving for England, where he was to practice law. *Library of Congress.*

This photo was most likely taken after 1925, the year that the Judah P. Benjamin Chapter of the United Daughters of the Confederacy purchased the Gamble Plantation. The property was donated to the State of Florida in 1949. *State Archives of Florida.*

FORT JEFFERSON

Dry Tortugas National Park
https://www.nps.gov/drto/index.htm

Dry Tortugas National Park, located approximately seventy miles from Key West, is the location of Fort Jefferson. Visitors may access the park via boat or seaplane. The park does have an entrance fee allowing for seven consecutive days of access, in addition to any transportation costs.

During the Civil War, the unfinished fort served as a Union outpost. Navy ships participating in the East Gulf Blockading Squadron used it as a supply depot. At its busiest, the fort was home to more than two thousand people, including soldiers and their families, prisoners and laborers. In 1865, Samuel Arnold, Michael O'Laughlen, Edman Spangler and Samuel A. Mudd were convicted in the Lincoln assassination plot. While spared the gallows, the four men were sentenced to prison at Fort Jefferson. Michael O'Laughlen was to die at Fort Jefferson from yellow fever. Mudd was to take a lead medical role during an 1867 outbreak. For his role in saving the lives of hundreds of men, President Andrew Johnson granted a pardon to Mudd in 1869.

A visitor stands at the plaque recognizing the captivity of Abraham Lincoln assassination conspirator Samuel A. Mudd. While at Fort Jefferson, Mudd attempted escape once. He went on to assist sick patients during a yellow fever outbreak and received parole from President Andrew Johnson. *State Archives of Florida.*

OUT-OF-STATE MONUMENTS TO FLORIDA TROOPS

Civil War enthusiasts are highly engaged. We read voraciously, keep up with websites and blogs and often travel to witness the actual terrain we have read so much about. For those with an interest in Florida troops and their contributions to the war, it is important to know that markers to Florida troops are located on several distant battlefields. Be sure to visit them in your travels.[226]

CHICKAMAUGA

Lafayette Road
Chickamauga and Chattanooga National Military Park
https://www.nps.gov/chch/index.htm

The Battle of Chickamauga, fought September 19–20, 1863, was an extremely bloody one. Casualties totaled more than 35,000. The seven companies of Florida soldiers lost more than 550 men, dead, wounded or missing. The monument to Florida troops was constructed in 1912–13 and dedicated in May 1913. The impressive monument is twenty-four feet tall and eighteen feet square. The monument is constructed of granite in a

temple design, open on all four sides with a bronze statue in the center. Critics have noted that a monument later constructed in Jacksonville by the same design firm bore a striking resemblance to this one.[227]

Standing tall in the bright Georgia sun, this monument, dedicated in 1913 on the Chickamauga battlefield, honors the more than 550 casualties suffered by Florida troops during the battle. *Carol M. Highsmith Archive, Library of Congress.*

FRANKLIN

McGavock Confederate Cemetery
1345 Carnton Lane
https://mcgavockcemetery.org/

On November 30, 1864, the bloody Battle of Franklin occurred, leading to more than nine thousand combined casualties, of which more than six thousand were Confederate. In 1866, the McGavock family donated approximately two acres of land to create a cemetery to the Southern dead. In the following years, nearly 1,500 Confederate soldiers were buried here. The cemetery contains two sections, and each section contains separate areas, divided by Confederate state. The section for Florida contains a five-foot-tall, shaft-shaped monument and the remains of four soldiers.

GETTYSBURG

West Confederate Avenue
Gettysburg National Military Park
https://www.nps.gov/gett/index.htm

Led by Colonel David Lang, the Florida Brigade, Second, Fifth, and Eighth Infantry Regiments, took part in much of the bloodiest fighting on July 2 and 3, 1863, including participating in Pickett's Charge, the ill-fated final attempt to break Union lines. The relatively modern monument,

Erected in 1963 in recognition of the three regiments of Florida troops that fought at Gettysburg, the monument has multiple references to the number three: the number of panels, the number of steps and the number of stars. Colonel David Lang led the Florida Brigade during the battle. *State Archives of Florida.*

dedicated in 1963, features multiple references to the three regiments who fought at Gettysburg. These include the three stars above the inscription, the three panels of the monument and the three steps on the monument. The monument states that the Florida Brigade suffered 445 casualties, while a more modern assessment has lowered that to just under 350. No matter the number, the Florida Brigade suffered an incredibly high percentage of men killed, wounded, captured or missing.[228]

MANASSAS

Grovetown Confederate Cemetery
Manassas National Battlefield Park
https://www.nps.gov/places/000/groveton-confederate-cemetery.htm

Groveton Confederate Cemetery is the final resting place of approximately five hundred unknown Confederate dead, most casualties of the Battle of Second Manassas. Grave markers identify only two individuals. The Second, Fifth and Eighth Florida Infantries were held in reserve during the battle but did suffer casualties because of artillery fire hitting their position. It is possible some of the buried dead were from these regiments. The cemetery consists of a sixteen-foot-tall main monument made of a combination of granite and marble. Surrounding this are fourteen smaller white marble shafts representing eleven seceded states and three border states. The Groveton and Bull Run Memorial Association began organization of the cemetery, a task that the Bull Run chapter of the Virginia division of the United Daughters of the Confederacy completed in 1904.[229]

VICKSBURG

South Confederate Avenue
Vicksburg National Military Park
https://www.nps.gov/vick/index.htm

One can argue that the Battle of Vicksburg was perhaps more important in determining the fate of the Confederacy than the Battle of Gettysburg. In 1954, the United Daughters of the Confederacy erected a monument in recognition of the First, Third, and Fourth Florida Infantry regiments who served under Joseph E. Johnston at Vicksburg. Students of the Siege of Vicksburg might question why there is a monument to Florida troops despite their nonparticipation in the siege. Past park superintendent James R. McConghie explained this anomaly:

The Florida Division of the United Daughters of the Confederacy instigated a movement to have a monument placed in the Vicksburg National Military Park as a memorial to the Florida troops who served with Johnson's [sic] *Army. In the past, other organizations have placed small memorials in the southern section of the park to their troops even though they may not have served at Vicksburg.*[230]

WINCHESTER

305 Boscawen Street
Winchester, VA
Mount Hebron Cemetery
https://www.mthebroncemetery.org/confederate-cemetery.html

Within the boundaries of the larger Mount Hebron Cemetery lies the Stonewall Confederate Cemetery. This cemetery contains the remains of 2,575 Confederate soldiers who died in local battlefields and hospitals and were never returned home. Each state has a separate location around a large monument dedicated to the 829 unknown soldiers buried there. The Florida section is located adjacent to the monument to the unknowns. There are thirty-eight Florida soldiers interred around a larger granite obelisk that the United Daughters of the Confederacy installed in 1902.[231]

Notes

Introduction

1. Quoted in Frederick P. Gaske, *Florida Civil War Heritage Trail* (Tallahassee, FL: Florida Association of Museums, n.d.), 2.
2. The best resource on regiments and soldiers from Florida who fought in the Civil War is David Hartman and David Coles, *Biographical Roster of Florida's Confederate and Union Troops, 1861–1865*, 6 vols. (Wilmington, NC: Broadfoot Publishing, 1995.)
3. United States War Department, *War of the Rebellion: Official Records of the Union and Confederate Armies*, series 1, vol. 6 (Washington, D.C.: United States Government Printing Office, 1889), 406. (Hereafter cited as *ORA*. All future references are to series 1 unless otherwise noted.)
4. Tyler Campbell, "The First Florida Cavalry (US): Union Enlistment in the Civil War's Southern Periphery" (master's thesis, University of Central Florida, 2018), 2.
5. Larry Eugene Rivers, *Slavery in Florida: Territorial Days to Emancipation* (Gainesville, FL: University Press of Florida, 2000), 232–35. For information on individual Florida regiments, readers should reference Hartman and Coles, *Biographical Roster*.
6. For a critical review of the Dunning School literature, please see John David Smith and J. Vincent Lowery, eds., *The Dunning School: Historians, Race, and the Meaning of Reconstruction* (Lexington, KY: University Press of Kentucky, 2013).

7. Jonathan M. Berkey, review of *Florida's Civil War: Terrible Sacrifices*, by Tracy J. Revels, *Journal of Southern History* 84, no. 1 (February 2018): 163–64.

8. James N. Denham, review of *Slavery in Florida: Territorial Days to Emancipation*, by Larry Eugene Rivers, *American Historical Review* 106 (December 2001): 1802–3. Other positive reviews include Randolph B. Campbell, *Journal of American History* 88 (December 2001): 1070–71, and Anthony E. Kaye, *Civil War History* 48 (March 2002): 89–90.

9. Michael C. Hardy, "Biographies on Florida's Confederate Generals," *Looking for the Confederate War* (blog), December 9, 2020, http://michaelchardy.blogspot.com/2020/12/biographies-on-floridas-confederate.html.

10. Esther Hill Hawks Papers, Library of Congress, accessed January 12, 2022, https://www.loc.gov/item/mm79025304/.

Chapter 1

11. Joseph H. Parks, *General Edmund Kirby Smith, C.S.A.* (Baton Rouge, LA: Louisiana State University Press, 1982), 104.

12. John E. Johns, *Florida during the Civil War* (Gainesville, FL: University Press of Florida, 1963), 7–8.

13. Quoted in Johns, *Florida during the Civil War*, 10.

14. Dorothy Dodd, "The Secession Movement in Florida 1850–1861 Part II," *Florida Historical Quarterly* 12 (October 1933): 51; Johns, *Florida during the Civil War*, 10; Ralph A. Wooster, "The Florida Secession Convention," *Florida Historical Quarterly* 36 (April 1958): 373.

15. Quoted in Johns, *Florida during the Civil War*, 11.

16. George F. Pearce, *Pensacola during the Civil War: A Thorn in the Side of the Confederacy* (Gainesville, FL: University Press of Florida, 2000), 4.

17. Quoted in John Reiger, "Secession of Florida from the Union—A Minority Decision?" *Florida Historical Quarterly* 46 (April 1968): 362.

18. Dodd, "Secession Movement in Florida," 54–55; Johns, *Florida during the Civil War*, 5.

19. Wooster, "Florida Secession Convention," 374.

20. Ibid., 374–76.

21. Johns, *Florida during the Civil War*, 15.

22. Dodd, "Secession Movement in Florida," 59–61; Johns, *Florida during the Civil War*, 15–17; Wooster, "Florida Secession Convention," 376.

23. Johns, *Florida during the Civil War*, 17; Reiger, "Secession of Florida," 365; Edmund Ruffin, "Account of the Florida Secession Convention: A Diary." *Florida Historical Quarterly* 12 (October 1933): 71.
24. Johns, *Florida during the Civil War*, 17; Ruffin, "Account," 71–72.
25. Dodd, "Secession Movement in Florida," 61; Johns, *Florida during the Civil War*, 17; Ruffin, "Account," 72–73; Wooster, "Florida Secession Convention," 376–77.
26. Johns, *Florida during the Civil War*, 17–18; Wooster, "Florida Secession Convention," 377.
27. Quoted in Johns, *Florida during the Civil War*, 18–19; Pearce, *Pensacola*, 7–8; Reiger, "Secession of Florida," 366.
28. Johns, *Florida during the Civil War*, 19.
29. Ibid., 20; Reiger, "Secession of Florida," 366–67.
30. Quoted in Reiger, "Secession of Florida," 367–68.
31. Quoted in Johns, *Florida during the Civil War*, 1.
32. Dodd, "Secession Movement in Florida," 62–63; Reiger, "Secession of Florida," 366.

Chapter 2

33. *St. Augustine Examiner*, November 24, 1860, and December 29, 1860.
34. *ORA*, vol. 1, 332.
35. *ORA*, vol. 1, 333.
36. Mrs. Frances Kirby Smith to Edmund Kirby Smith, January 11, 1860, quoted in Parks, *General Edmund Kirby Smith*, 104.
37. Paul Taylor, *Discovering the Civil War in Florida: A Reader and Guide*, 2nd ed. (Sarasota, FL: Pineapple Press, 2012), 147.
38. United States War Department, *Official Records of the Union and Confederate Navies* (Washington, D.C.: United States Government Printing Office, 1894–1922): volume 12, pages 207–08. (Hereafter cited as *ORN*.)
39. Jacqueline K. Fretwell, ed., *Civil War Times in St. Augustine* (Port Salerno, FL: Florida Classics Library, 1988), 23–24.
40. *ORA*, vol. 6, 406.
41. Mrs. Frances Kirby Smith to Edmund Kirby Smith, undated letter quoted in Parks, *General Edmund Kirby Smith*, 123.
42. *ORA*, vol. 12, 595–97.

Chapter 3

43. Robert A. Taylor, *Rebel Storehouse: Florida's Contribution to the Confederacy* (Tuscaloosa: University of Alabama Press, 2003), 91.

44. Robert A. Taylor, "Rebel Beef: Florida Cattle and the Confederate Army, 1862–1864," *Florida Historical Quarterly* 67 (July 1988), 31.

45. Ibid.

46. Joe A. Akerman Jr. and J. Mark Akerman, *Jacob Summerlin: King of the Crackers* (Cocoa: Florida Historical Society Press, 2004), 4; Taylor, *Rebel Storehouse*, 91.

47. Akerman and Akerman, *Jacob Summerlin*, 33.

48. Ibid., 31.

49. Ibid., 43.

50. 1860 U.S. Census, population schedule. NARA microfilm publication M653, 1,438 rolls. Washington, D.C.: National Archives and Records Administration.

51. Akerman and Akerman, *Jacob Summerlin*, 44–47; Cantor Brown Jr., "Tampa's James McKay and the Frustration of Confederate Cattle-Supply Operations in South Florida," *Florida Historical Quarterly* 70 (April 1992), 412–15.

52. Akerman and Akerman, *Jacob Summerlin*, 49.

53. Ibid., 50–51.

54. William Watson Davis, *The Civil War and Reconstruction in Florida* (New York: Columbia University Press, 1913), 270–71.

55. Taylor, *Rebel Beef*, 17.

56. Akerman and Akerman, 50–51; Taylor, *Rebel Storehouse*, 92–94.

57. Taylor, *Rebel Storehouse*, 94–95.

58. Ibid., 96–97.

59. Robert A. Taylor, "Cow Cavalry: Munnerlyn's Battalion in Florida, 1864–1865," *Florida Historical Quarterly* 65 (October 1986), 196; Robert A. Taylor, "A Problem of Supply: Pleasant White and Florida's Cow Cavalry," in *Divided We Fall: Essays on Confederate Nation-Building*, ed. John M. Belohlavek and Lewis N. Wynne (St. Leo, FL: St. Leo College Press, 1991), 178; Taylor, *Rebel Beef*, 15–16.

60. Taylor, *Rebel Beef*, 17; Taylor, *Rebel Storehouse*, 96–97.

61. Taylor, *Rebel Storehouse*, 100.

62. Ibid., 100–1.

63. Taylor, *Rebel Beef*, 18–19; Taylor, *Rebel Storehouse*, 101–2.

64. Taylor, *Rebel Beef*, 19; Taylor, *Rebel Storehouse*, 101–2.

65. Taylor, *Rebel Storehouse*, 103–4.

66. Taylor, *Rebel Beef*, 19–20; Taylor, *Problem*, 180–81; Taylor, *Rebel Storehouse*, 103–4.
67. Johns, *Florida during the Civil War*, 191; Taylor, *Rebel Beef*, 21; Taylor, *Rebel Storehouse*, 106.
68. Taylor, *Rebel Beef*, 21–22.
69. Ibid., 22; Taylor, *Rebel Storehouse*, 107.
70. *ORA*, series 4, vol. 2, 968; Taylor, *Rebel Beef*, 25; Taylor, *Rebel Storehouse*, 111.
71. Taylor, *Rebel Beef*, 24; Taylor, *Rebel Storehouse*, 110.
72. Joseph E. Johnston, *Narrative of Military Actions during the Late War Between the States* (Bloomington: Indiana University Press, 1959), 263–66.
73. Taylor, *Rebel Storehouse*, 110.
74. Taylor, *Rebel Beef*, 27–28.
75. Ibid., 29–30; Taylor, *Rebel Storehouse*, 122–23.
76. Taylor, *Cow Cavalry*, 197.
77. Ibid., 197–98.
78. Ibid., 198–99, Hartman and Coles, *Biographical Roster*, vol. 5, 2008–09.
79. Hartman and Coles, *Biographical Roster*, vol. 4, 1368–77; *ORA*, vol. 6, 133 and vol. 23, part 1, 173; Taylor, *Cow Cavalry*, 199.
80. Hartman and Coles, *Biographical Roster*, vol. 5, 2010–18; Taylor, *Cow Cavalry*, 201.
81. Taylor, *Cow Cavalry*, 202.
82. For a concise review of the Brooksville raid, see Michael C. Hardy and Robert M. Hardy, *A Heinous Sin: The 1864 Brooksville-Bayport Raid* (self-published, Lulu, 2009); Hartman and Coles, vol. 5, 2019–40; Taylor, *Cow Cavalry*, 204–6.
83. Hartman and Coles, *Biographical Roster*, vol. 5, 2041–44; Taylor, *Cow Cavalry*, 206–7.
84. Hartman and Coles, *Biographical Roster*, vol. 5, 2056–57; Taylor, *Cow Cavalry*, 207.
85. Hartman and Coles, *Biographical Roster*, vol. 5, 2058; Taylor, *Cow Cavalry*, 207.
86. Hartman and Coles, *Biographical Roster*, vol. 5, 2045–49; Taylor, *Cow Cavalry*, 207–8.
87. Hartman and Coles, *Biographical Roster*, vol. 5, 2050–55; Taylor, *Cow Cavalry*, 210.
88. Taylor, *Cow Cavalry*, 210.
89. *ORA*, vol. 49, 40–43; Taylor, *Cow Cavalry*, 211.
90. Rodney E. Dillon Jr., "The Battle of Fort Meyers," *Tampa Bay History* 5, no. 2, article 4: 2, https://scholarcommons.usf.edu/tampabayhistory/vol5/iss2/4.
91. Dillon, "Battle of Fort Meyers," 5; Taylor, *Cow Cavalry*, 211–12.
92. Dillon, "Battle of Fort Meyers," 5.

93. Ibid., 5; *ORA*, vol. 49, part 1, 53–54.

94. Ibid.

95. Ibid.

96. Dillon, "Battle of Fort Meyers," 7; *ORA*, vol. 49, part 1, 53–54.

97. Taylor, *Rebel Beef*, 31; Taylor, *Rebel Storehouse*, 126 and 131–32.

Chapter 4

98. United States Census Office and General Land Office, 1860 U.S. Census for Central Florida.

99. Michael G. Schene, *Hopes, Dreams, and Promises: A History of Volusia County, Florida* (Daytona Beach, FL: News-Journal, 1976), 65; 1860 U.S. census, population schedule.

100. David J. Coles, "Volusia County: The Land Warfare, 1861–1865," in *The Civil War in Volusia County: A Symposium April 24–26, 1987* (Daytona Beach, FL: Halifax Historical Society, 1987), 40–41; Hartman and Coles, *Biographical Roster*, vol. 1, 208–18 and 273–84.

101. Coles, "Volusia County: The Land Warfare," 39.

102. Harold Cardwell, "New Smyrna: Confederacy's Keyhole through the Union Blockade," in *Civil War in Volusia County*, 15; E. Garrett Youngblood, "Ponce de Leon Inlet Has Long Been a Problem for Seafarers," *Orlando Sentinel*, November 8, 2000, https://www.orlandosentinel.com/news/os-xpm-2000-11-08-0011080486-story.html.

103. Thomas Graham, "Naval Activities at Mosquito Inlet," in *Civil War in Volusia County*, 23–24.

104. *ORA*, vol. 6, 370.

105. *ORN*, vol. 12, 646–47.

106. Quoted in T.E. Fitzgerald, *Volusia County Past and Present* (Daytona Beach, FL: Observer Press, 1937), 91–92.

107. *ORN*, vol. 12, 648 and 651.

108. Ibid., 646.

109. Ibid., 655–56 and 768.

110. *ORN*, vol. 13, 156.

111. Quoted in Fitzgerald, *Volusia County*, 93–94.

112. *ORN*, vol. 17, 529.

113. Graham, "Naval Activities," 31.

114. Quoted in Jo Anne Sikes and Sandy Sammons, *Two Early Doctors* (Edgewater, FL: n.p., n.d.), 6.

115. Ibid., 11.

116. Charles H. Coe, "The Late Dr. John Milton Hawks," *Daytona Beach (FL) Observer*, August 30, 1941.

117. Quoted in John Milton Hawks, "An 1870 Itinerary from St. Augustine to Miami," *Florida Historical Quarterly* 18 (January 1940): 210.

118. Quoted in Sikes and Sammons, *Two Early Doctors*, 20.

119. Denny Bowden, "Freemanville, Volusia's 1st African-American Community," *Volusia History—Retracing the Past*, November 6, 2013, https:// volusiahistory.wordpress.com/2013/11/06/freemanville-volusias-1st-african-american-community/.

120. Schene, *Hopes, Dreams, and Promises*, 80.

121. Hawks, "St. Augustine to Miami," 210–11.

122. Quoted in Gerald Schwartz, ed., *A Woman Doctor's Civil War: Esther Hill Hawks' Diary* (Columbia: University of South Carolina Press, 1984), 25.

123. Quoted in Sikes and Sammons, *Two Early Doctors*, 29.

124. Bowden, "Freemanville."

125. Ianthe Bond Hebel, *Captain Simmons Bennett: An Early Pioneer and the Halifax River*, five-page undated typescript.

126. Robert Redd, *New Smyrna Beach: Postcard History Series* (Charleston, SC: Arcadia Publishing, 2016), 10.

127. Ponce Inlet Lighthouse and Museum, "Lighthouse Keepers," accessed December 9, 2021, https://www.ponceinlet.org/Lighthouse-Keepers-6-95.html.

Chapter 5

128. *ORA*, vol. 35, part 2, 286–87.

129. Mark Boyd, "The Battle of Marianna," *Florida Historical Quarterly* 29 (April 1951): 225–27.

130. *ORA*, vol. 35, part 2, 283.

131. Boyd, "Marianna," 227.

132. *ORA*, vol. 35, part 1, 443.

133. Ibid., 444.

134. Ibid., 445.

135. Quoted in St. Luke's Episcopal Church, "The St. Luke's Bible: A Legend about the Battle of Marianna, Florida," accessed December 15, 2021, https://www.stlukesmarianna.org/content.cfm?id=314.

136. *ORA*, vol. 35, part 1, 445.

137. Boyd, "Marianna," 235.

138. Ibid., 238.

139. Ibid.

140. For information on where this phrase came from, see John J. Dickison, "Military History of Florida," in *Confederate Military History*, ed. Clement Evans, vol. 11, part 2 (Atlanta: Confederate Publishing, 1898), 114.

141. William B. Lees and Frederick P. Gaske, *Recalling Deeds Immortal: Florida's Monuments to the Civil War* (Gainesville: University Press of Florida, 2014), 208–11; W. Stuart Towns. "Honoring the Confederacy in Northwest Florida: The Confederate Monument Ritual," *Florida Historical Quarterly* 57 (October 1978): 210–11.

Chapter 6

142. David J. Coles, "Florida's Seed Corn: The History of the West Florida Seminary during the Civil War," *Florida Historical Quarterly* 77 (Winter 1999): 285.

143. Mark F. Boyd, "Joint Operations of the Federal Army and Navy Near St. Marks, Florida, March 1865," *Florida Historical Quarterly* 29 (October 1950): 117; Taylor, *Discovering the Civil War*, 79.

144. Florida State University, "History," accessed February 8, 2022, https://www.fsu.edu/about/history.html.

145. Coles, "Florida's Seed Corn," 285–86.

146. Ibid., 287.

147. Ibid., 288.

148. Taylor, *Discovering the Civil War, 80.*

149. Ibid.

150. Boyd, "Joint Operations," 117; Coles, "Florida's Seed Corn," 289. Readers will note that some sources list the name of V.M. Johnson, while others cite V.M. Johnston.

151. James Lee Conrad, *The Young Lions: Confederate Cadets at War* (Mechanicsburg, PA: Stackpole Books, 1997), 157.

152. For a good review of military schools in the Confederate states, please see Conrad, *The Young Lions.*

153. Quoted in Coles, "Florida's Seed Corn," 293–94.

154. Ibid., 294.

155. Ibid., 296–97.

156. Ellen Call Long, *Florida Breezes; or Florida, New and Old* (Gainesville: University Press of Florida, 1962): 375.

157. Quoted in Coles, "Florida's Seed Corn," 296.
158. David James Coles, "Far from Fields of Glory: Military Operations in Florida during the Civil War 1864–1865" (PhD diss., Florida State University, 1996): 336–37.
159. James M. Dancy, "Reminiscences of the Civil War," *Florida Historical Quarterly* 37 (July 1958): 82.
160. Quoted in Coles, "Florida's Seed Corn," 300.
161. Ibid., 301.
162. Ibid., 302.
163. Ibid., 305.
164. Ibid., 305–6.
165. Ibid., 305–6.
166. Ibid., 306–8.
167. Ibid., 309.
168. Lees and Gaske, *Recalling Deeds Immortal*, 211–18.

Chapter 7

169. Geneva Historical and Genealogical Society, *Geneva & the Lincoln Conspiracy: The Story of Lewis Thornton Powell* (Geneva, FL: M and M Publishing, 2021): 9–10; Leon O. Prior, "Lewis Payne, Pawn of John Wilkes Booth," *Florida Historical Quarterly* 43 (July 1964): 2.
170. Prior, "Lewis Payne," 2–3.
171. Prior, "Lewis Payne," 3–7.
172. Geneva, *Geneva & the Lincoln Conspiracy*, 17.
173. Prior, "Lewis Payne," 8–9.
174. Ibid., 9.
175. Ibid., 9–10.
176. Ibid., 10–12.
177. Wesley Harris, "Why Lewis Powell's Pistol Failed to Fire," *Surratt Currier* 36 (November 2011): 3–5; Michael W. Kaufman, *American Brutus: John Wilkes Booth and the Lincoln Conspiracies* (New York: Random House, 2004): 22–24; Prior, "Lewis Payne," 12–14; James L. Swanson, *Manhunt: The 12-Day Chase for Lincoln's Killer* (New York: Harper Collins, 2006): 51–61.
178. Prior, "Lewis Payne," 14.
179. Prior, "Lewis Payne," 15–16; for the full text of William E. Doster's closing argument in defense of Lewis Powell, see William E. Doster, "William E. Doster's Defense of Lewis Powell," *Famous Trials by Professor*

Douglas O. Linder, University of Missouri–Kansas City School of Law, accessed October 27, 2021, https://famous-trials.com/lincoln/2177-defenseofpowell.

180. Kaufman, *American Brutus*, 369.

181. Geneva, *Geneva & the Lincoln Conspiracy*, 19–33; Kaufman, *American Brutus*, 373–74; Prior, "Lewis Payne," 18–19.

182. Betty J. Ownsbey, *Alias "Paine": Lewis Thornton Powell, the Mystery Man of the Lincoln Conspiracy* (Jefferson, NC: McFarland, 2015); Betty J. Ownsbey, "And Now—The Rest of the Story: The Search for the Rest of the Remains of Lewis 'Paine' Powell," *Surratt Courier* 37 (October 2012): 3–6; St. Paul's Rock Creek Cemetery, "Notable Burials," accessed October 28, 2021, https://rockcreekcemetery.org/notable-burials/.

183. Geneva, *Geneva and the Lincoln Conspiracy*, 37–38; Glenwood Cemetery, "Notables," accessed October 28, 2021, https://www.theglenwoodcemetery.com/notables/; Ownsbey, "And Now," 3–6; Ownsbey, *Alias "Paine,"* 188–90; Dave Taylor, "The National Museum of Health and Medicine and the Lincoln Assassination," *Lincoln Conspirators*, June 1, 2014, https://lincolnconspirators.com/2014/06/01/the-national-museum-of-health-and-medicine-and-the-lincoln-assassination/.

184. Geneva, *Geneva & the Lincoln Conspiracy*, 37–38; National Park Service, "Native American Graves Protection and Repatriation Act," last updated November 22, 2019, https://www.nps.gov/subjecls/nagpra/index.htm; Jim Robison, "Infamous Floridian's Skull to Remain at Smithsonian," *Orlando Sentinel*, May 9, 1993.

185. Prior, "Lewis Payne," 18–19.

186. Ibid., 19–20.

187. Robison, "Infamous Floridian."

188. Ibid.

189. Geneva, *Geneva & the Lincoln Conspiracy*, 37–38; Jim Robison, "Lincoln Conspirator's Remains Buried in Seminole County," *Orlando Sentinel*, November 13, 1994.

190. Geneva Historical and Genealogical Society, *The Making of a Village: A History of Geneva, Florida* (Geneva, FL: M and M Publishing, 2012): 71.

191. Edward Steers Jr., *His Name Is Still Mudd: The Case against Dr. Samuel Alexander Mudd* (Gettysburg, PA: Thomas Publications, 1997): 3.

192. Quoted in Edward Steers Jr., *Blood on the Moon: The Assassination of Abraham Lincoln* (Lexington: University Press of Kentucky, 2001): 154; Steers, *His Name*, 40.

193. Steers, *His Name*, 29.

194. Ibid., 106–15.

195. Ibid., 60.

196. Ibid.

197. Kaufman, *American Brutus*, 369; Steers, *Blood on the Moon*, 227.

198. National Park Service, "Dry Tortugas National Park, Florida," last updated June 30, 2021, https://www.nps.gov/drto/index.htm; National Park Service, "National Register of Historic Places Inventory Form: Fort Jefferson National Monument," accessed November 10, 2021, https://catalog.archives.gov/id/77843330.

199. Kat Long, "How Samuel Mudd Went from Lincoln Conspirator to Medical Savior," *Smithsonian*, April 14, 2015, https://www.smithsonianmag.com/history/how-samuel-mudd-went-lincoln-conspirator-medical-savior-180954980/.

200. Quoted in Steers, *Blood on the Moon*, 236; Dave Taylor, "The Escape Attempt of Dr. Mudd," *Surratt Courier* 37 (November 2012): 3.

201. Taylor, "Escape Attempt," 4.

202. Quoted in Steers, *Blood on the Moon*, 238.

203. Steers, *Blood on the Moon*, 236–39; Taylor, "Escape Attempt," 3–5.

204. Long, "How Samuel Mudd"; Steers, *Blood on the Moon*, 240.

205. Long, "How Samuel Mudd."

206. Quoted in Long, "How Samuel Mudd."

207. Steers, *Blood on the Moon*, 241–42.

208. Ibid., 242.

209. Ibid.

210. National Park Service, "National Register of Historic Places Inventory Form: Fort Jefferson National Monument," accessed November 10, 2021, https://catalog.archives.gov/id/77843330. See application continuation sheet #5.

Chapter 8

211. Many museums will offer this printed booklet free of charge. Failing that, as of the writing of this book, the State of Florida Division of Historical Resources offers a free downloadable copy. Please visit https://dos.myflorida.com/historical/preservation/heritage-trails/civil-war-heritage-trail/.

212. For readers interested in a full treatment of the Battle of Olustee, please see Robert P Broadwater, *The Battle of Olustee, 1864: The Final Union Attempt to Seize Florida* (Jefferson, NC: McFarland Publishing, 2006); William H.

Nulty, *Confederate Florida: The Road to Olustee* (Tuscaloosa: University of Alabama Press, 1994); Daniel L. Schafer, *Thunder on the River: The Civil War in Northeast Florida* (Gainesville: University Press of Florida, 2010).

213. Lees and Gaske, *Recalling Deeds Immortal*, 196–97.

214. Ibid., 199–200.

215. U.S. Department of Veterans Affairs National Cemetery Administration, "Barrancas National Cemetery," last updated December 10, 2019, https://www.cem.va.gov/cems/nchp/barrancas.asp.

216. Gaske, *Florida Civil War Heritage Trail*, 19; St. Luke's Episcopal Church, "Cemetery," accessed January 13, 2022, https://www.stlukesmarianna.org/content.cfm?id=316.

217. There is no biography of Colonel David Lang. Readers are referred to Bertram H. Groene, ed., "The Civil War Letters of Colonel David Lang," *Florida Historical Quarterly* 54 (January 1976): 340–66. Readers are also referred to any of the many works detailing Pickett's charge at the Battle of Gettysburg. Cemetery information is available at City of Tallahassee, "Old City Cemetery," https://www.talgov.com/realestate/res-coc-oldcity.aspx.

218. Mandarin Museum, "Maple Leaf," *Mandarin Museum and Historical Society*, accessed November 22, 2021, https://www.mandarinmuseum.net/mandarin-history/maple-leaf; Maple Leaf Shipwreck, "Maple Leaf Shipwreck: An Extraordinary Civil War American Shipwreck," accessed November 22, 2021, http://www.mapleleafshipwreck.com/index.htm.

219. Florida Memory, "Old Confederate Soldiers and Sailors Home," accessed November 23, 2021, https://www.floridamemory.com/discover/historical_records/confedhome/.

220. *ORA*, vol. 6, 96.

221. City of Palatka, "Bronson-Mulholland House," accessed November 23, 2021, https://www.palatka-fl.gov/239/Bronson-Mulholland-House.

222. Robert Redd, *St. Augustine and the Civil War* (Charleston, SC: The History Press, 2014): 82–87.

223. For a very short biographical sketch of James B. Parramore, see Betty Jo Stockton, "James B. Parramore—Mayor of Orlando 1897–1902," *Buried Treasures: Central Florida Genealogical Society, Inc.* 39: (Fall 2007), 87, https://cfgs.org/wp-content/uploads/files/quarterly/bt200712_cfgs_quarterly_vol_39-4.pdf.

224. Roger T. Grange Jr. and Dorothy L. Moore, *Smyrnea Settlement: Archaeology & History of an 18th Century British Plantation in East Florida* (New Smyrna Beach, FL: New Smyrna Museum of History, 2016): 16.

Interested readers may contact the museum for a physical copy of this booklet or view it online at the museum website: https://www.nsbhistory. org/smyrnea-settlement/.

225. National Register of Historic Places, "Judah P. Benjamin Memorial (Gamble House)," accessed January 25, 2022, https://catalog.archives. gov/id/77843018.

226. The most complete history of monuments in and related to Florida is Lees and Gaske, *Recalling Deeds Immortal*.

227. Ibid., 239–43.

228. Groene, "Civil War Letters of Colonel David Lang."

229. Lees and Gaske, *Recalling Deeds Immortal*, 238–39.

230. Ibid., 248.

231. Ibid., *Recalling Deeds Immortal*, 235–38; Mount Hebron Cemetery, "Stonewall Confederate Cemetery," accessed January 25, 2022, https:// www.mthebroncemetery.org/confederate-cemetery.html.

BIBLIOGRAPHY

Articles

Bearss, Edwin C. "Federal Expedition against Saint Marks Ends at Natural Bridge." *Florida Historical Quarterly* 45 (April 1967): 369–90.

Berkey, Jonathan M. Review of *Florida's Civil War: Terrible Sacrifices*, by Tracy J. Revels, *Journal of Southern History* 84, no. 1 (February 2018): 163–64.

Bittle, George C. "Florida Prepares for War, 1860–1861." *Florida Historical Quarterly* 51 (October 1972): 143–52.

Boyd, Mark F. "The Battle of Marianna." *Florida Historical Quarterly* 29 (April 1951): 225–42.

———. "Joint Operations of the Federal Army and Navy near St. Marks, Florida, March 1865." *Florida Historical Quarterly* 29 (October 1950): 96–24.

Brown, Cantor, Jr. "Tampa's James McKay and the Frustration of Confederate Cattle-Supply Operations in South Florida." *Florida Historical Quarterly* 70 (April 1992): 409–33.

Chapman, Fanny B. "The Battle at Marianna, Fla." *Confederate Veteran* 19 (October 1911): 483–84.

Clarke, Robert L. "Northern Plans for the Economic Invasion of Florida, 1862–1865." *Florida Historical Quarterly* 28 (April 1950): 262–70.

Coe, Charles, H. "The Late Dr. John Milton Hawks." *Daytona Beach (FL) Observer*, August 30, 1941.

Coles, David J. "Florida's Seed Corn: The History of the West Florida Seminary during the Civil War." *Florida Historical Quarterly* 77 (Winter 1999): 283–319.

Coles, David J., and Robert Bruce Graetz. "The Garnet and Gray: West Florida Seminary in the Civil War." *Florida State: The Magazine of the Florida State University Alumni Association* (April 1986): 2–4.

Cortada, James W. "Florida's Relations with Cuba during the Civil War." *Florida Historical Quarterly* 59 (July 1980): 42–52.

Dancy, James M. "Reminiscences of the Civil War." *Florida Historical Quarterly* 37 (July 1958): 66–89.

Denham, James N. Review of *Slavery in Florida: Territorial Days to Emancipation*, by Larry Eugene Rivers. *American Historical Review* 106 (December 2001): 1802–3.

Dillon, Rodney E., Jr. "The Battle of Fort Myers." *Tampa Bay History* 5, no. 2, article 4: 2, https://scholarcommons.usf.edu/tampabayhistory/vol5/iss2/4.

Dodd, Dorothy. "The Secession Movement in Florida 1850—1861 Part I." *Florida Historical Quarterly* 12 (July 1933): 3–24.

———. "The Secession Movement in Florida 1850–1861 Part II." *Florida Historical Quarterly* 12 (October 1933): 45–66.

Dodd, William G. "Early Education in Tallahassee and the West Florida Seminary, Now Florida State University Part I." *Florida Historical Quarterly* 27 (July 1948): 1–27.

———. "Early Education in Tallahassee and the West Florida Seminary, Now Florida State University Part II." *Florida Historical Quarterly* 27 (October 1948): 157–79.

East, Omega. "St. Augustine during the Civil War." *Florida Historical Quarterly* 31 (October 1952): 75–91.

Falero, Frank, Jr. "Naval Engagements in Tampa Bay, 1862." *Florida Historical Quarterly* 46 (October 1967): 134–40.

Groene, Bertram H., ed. "The Civil War Letters of Colonel David Lang." *Florida Historical Quarterly* 54 (January 1976): 340–66.

Hawks, John Milton. "An 1870 Itinerary from St. Augustine to Miami." *Florida Historical Quarterly* 18 (January 1940): 204–15.

Lempel, Leonard. "Port Orange's (Almost) Forgotten Hamlet of Freemanville." *Halifax Herald* 29 (Winter 2011): 13–17.

Long, Kat. "How Samuel Mudd Went from Lincoln Conspirator to Medical Savior." *Smithsonian*, April 14, 2015. https://www.smithsonianmag.com/history/how-samuel-mudd-went-lincoln-conspirator-medical-savior-180954980/.

Lonn, Ella. "The Extent and Importance of Federal Naval Raids on Salt-Making in Florida, 1862–1865." *Florida Historical Quarterly* 10 (April 1932): 167–84.

Prior, Leon O. "Lewis Payne, Pawn of John Wilkes Booth." *Florida Historical Quarterly* 43 (July 1964): 1–20.

Reiger, John F. "Florida after Secession: Abandonment by the Confederacy and Its Consequences." *Florida Historical Quarterly* 50 (October 1971): 128–42.

———. "Secession of Florida from the Union—A Minority Decision?" *Florida Historical Quarterly* 46 (April 1968): 358–68.

Ruffin, Edmund. "Account of the Florida Secession Convention: A Diary." *Florida Historical Quarterly* 12 (October 1933): 67–76.

Still, William N., Jr. "A Naval Sieve: The Union Blockade in the Civil War." *Naval War College Review* 36, no. 3, article 5. https://digital-commons.usnwc.edu/nwc-review/vol36/iss3/5.

Stockton, Betty Jo. "James B. Parramore: Mayor of Orlando 1897–1902." *Buried Treasures: Central Florida Genealogical Society* 39 (Fall 2007): 87.

Surdman, David G. "The Union Navy's Blockade Reconsidered." *Naval War College Review* 51, no. 4, article 7. https://digital-commons.usnwc.edu/nwc-review/vol51/iss4/7.

Taylor, Robert A. "Cow Cavalry: Munnerlyn's Battalion in Florida, 1864–1865." *Florida Historical Quarterly:* 65 (October 1986): 196–214.

———. "Rebel Beef: Florida Cattle and the Confederate Army, 1862–1864." *Florida Historical Quarterly* 67 (July 1988): 15–31.

Towns, W. Stuart. "Honoring the Confederacy in Northwest Florida: The Confederate Monument Ritual." *Florida Historical Quarterly* 57 (October 1978): 205–12.

Waters, Zack C. "Florida's Confederate Guerillas: John W. Pearson and the Oklawaha Rangers." *Florida Historical Quarterly* 70 (October 1991): 133–49.

Wooster, Ralph A. "The Florida Secession Convention." *Florida Historical Quarterly* 36 (April 1958): 373–85.

Books

Akerman, Joe A., Jr., and J. Mark Akerman. *Jacob Summerlin: King of the Crackers.* Cocoa: Florida Historical Society Press, 2004.

Broadwater, Robert P. *The Battle of Olustee, 1864: The Final Union Attempt to Seize Florida.* Jefferson, NC: McFarland Publishing, 2006.

Cardwell, Harold D., Jr., and Priscilla D. Cardwell. *Port Orange: A Great Community.* Vol. 1. DeLand, FL: Tennant Printing, 2001.

Conrad, James Lee. *The Young Lions: Confederate Cadets at War.* Mechanicsburg, PA: Stackpole Books, 1997.

Davis, William Watson. *The Civil War and Reconstruction in Florida*. New York: Columbia University Press, 1913.

Dickison, John J. "Military History of Florida." In *Confederate Military History*, vol. 11, part 2, ed. Clement Evans (Atlanta, GA: Confederate Publishing, 1898).

Fitzgerald, T.E. *Volusia County: Past and Present*. Daytona Beach, FL: Observer Press, 1937.

Fretwell, Jacqueline K., ed. *Civil War Times in St. Augustine*. Port Salerno: Florida Classics Library, 1988.

Gannon, Michael, editor. *The New History of Florida*. Gainesville: University Press of Florida, 1996.

Gaske, Frederick P. *Florida Civil War Heritage Trail*. Tallahassee: Florida Association of Museums, n.d.

Geneva Historical and Genealogical Society. *Geneva & the Lincoln Conspiracy: The Story of Lewis Thornton Powell*. Geneva, FL: M and M Publishing, 2021.
———. *The Making of a Village: A History of Geneva, Florida*. Geneva, FL: M and M Publishing, 2012.

Gold, Pleasant Daniel. *History of Volusia County, Florida*. DeLand, FL: E.O. Painter Printing, 1927.

Grenier, Bob. *Central Florida's Civil War Veterans: Images of America*. Charleston, SC: Arcadia Publishing, 2014.

Hardy, Michael C., and Robert M. Hardy. *A Heinous Sin: The 1864 Brooksville-Bayport Raid*. Self-published, Lulu, 2009.

Hartman, David, and David Coles. *Biographical Roster of Florida's Confederate and Union Troops, 1861–1865*. 6 vols. Wilmington, NC: Broadfoot Publishing, 1995.

Johns, John E. *Florida during the Civil War*. Gainesville: University of Florida Press, 1963.

Johnston, Joseph E. *Narrative of Military Operations during the Late War Between the States*. Bloomington: Indiana University Press, 1959.

Kauffman, Michael W. *American Brutus: John Wilkes Booth and the Lincoln Conspiracies*. New York: Random House, 2004.

Lees, William B., and Frederick P. Gaske. *Recalling Deeds Immortal: Florida's Monuments to the Civil War*. Gainesville: University Press of Florida, 2014.

Long, Ellen Call. *Florida Breezes; or Florida, New and Old*. Gainesville: University Press of Florida, 1962.

Manucy, Albert, ed. *The History of Castillo de San Marcos & Fort Matanzas: From Contemporary Narratives and Letters*. National Park Service Source Book Series Number Three. Washington, D.C.: 1959.

Mattson, Robert A. *The Civil War Navy in Florida*. Palatka, FL: self-published, 2014.

Nulty, William H. *Confederate Florida: The Road to Olustee.* Tuscaloosa: University of Alabama Press, 1994.

Ownsbey, Betty J. *Alias "Paine": Lewis Thornton Powell, the Mystery Man of the Lincoln Conspiracy.* Jefferson, NC: McFarland, 2015.

Parks, Joseph H. *General Edmund Kirby Smith C.S.A.* Baton Rouge: Louisiana State University Press, 1982.

Pearce, George F. *Pensacola during the Civil War: A Thorn in the Side of the Confederacy.* Gainesville: University Press of Florida, 2000.

Redd, Robert. *New Smyrna Beach: Postcard History Series.* Charleston, SC: Arcadia Publishing, 2016.

———. *St. Augustine and the Civil War.* Charleston, SC: The History Press, 2014.

Revels, Tracy J. *Florida's Civil War: Terrible Sacrifices.* Macon: Mercer University Press, 2016.

———. *Grander in Her Daughters: Florida's Women during the Civil War.* Columbia: University of South Carolina Press, 2004.

Rivers, Larry Eugene. *Slavery in Florida: Territorial Days to Emancipation.* Gainesville: University Press of Florida, 2000.

Schafer, Daniel L. *Thunder on the River: The Civil War in Northeast Florida.* Gainesville: University Press of Florida, 2010.

Schene, Michael G. *Hopes, Dreams, and Promises: A History of Volusia County, Florida.* Daytona Beach, FL: News-Journal Corporation, 1976.

Schwartz, Gerald, ed. *A Woman Doctor's Civil War: Esther Hill Hawks' Diary.* Columbia: University of South Carolina Press, 1984.

Sheppard, Johnathan C. *By the Noble Daring of Her Sons: The Florida Brigade of the Army of Tennessee.* Tuscaloosa: University of Alabama Press, 2012.

Shofner, Jerrell H. *Nor Is It Over Yet: Florida in the Era of Reconstruction 1863–1877.* Gainesville: University Press of Florida, 1974.

Smith, John David, and J. Vincent Lowery, eds. *The Dunning School: Historians, Race, and the Meaning of Reconstruction.* Lexington: University Press of Kentucky, 2013.

Steers, Edward., Jr. *Blood on the Moon: The Assassination of Abraham Lincoln.* Lexington: University Press of Kentucky, 2001.

———. *His Name Is Still Mudd: The Case against Dr. Samuel Alexander Mudd.* Gettysburg, PA: Thomas Publications, 1997.

Swanson, James L. *Manhunt: The 12-Day Chase for Lincoln's Killer.* New York: HarperCollins, 2006.

Sweett, Zelia W. *New Smyrna, Florida in the Civil War.* New Smyrna Beach, FL: Volusia County Historical Commission, 1963.

Taylor, Paul. *Discovering the Civil War in Florida: A Reader and Guide*, 2nd ed. Sarasota, FL: Pineapple Press, 2012

Taylor, Robert A. "A Problem of Supply: Pleasant White and Florida's Cow Cavalry." In *Divided We Fall: Essays on Confederate Nation-Building*, edited by John M. Belohlavek and Lewis N. Wynne, 177–202. St. Leo, FL: St. Leo College Press, 1991.

———. *Rebel Storehouse: Florida's Contribution to the Confederacy.* Tuscaloosa: University of Alabama Press, 2003.

Tebeau, Charlton W., and William Marina. *A History of Florida.* Coral Gables, FL: University of Miami Press, 1999.

Waters, Zack C., and James C. Edmonds. *A Small but Spartan Band: The Florida Brigade in Lee's Army of Northern Virginia.* Tuscaloosa: University of Alabama Press, 2010.

Wynne, Lewis N., and Robert A. Taylor. *Florida in the Civil War.* Charleston, SC: Arcadia Publishing, 2001.

Wynne, Nick. *On This Day in Florida Civil War History.* Charleston, SC: The History Press, 2015.

Wynne, Nick, and Joe Crankshaw. *Florida Civil War Blockades: Battling for the Coast.* Charleston, SC: The History Press, 2011.

Miscellaneous

Bowden, Denny. "Freemanville, Volusia's 1st African-American Community." *Volusia's History—Retracing the Past*, November 6, 2013. https://volusiahistory.wordpress.com/2013/11/06/freemanville-volusias-1st-african-american-community/.

Campbell, Tyler. "The First Florida Cavalry (US): Union Enlistment in the Civil War's Southern Periphery." Master's thesis, University of Central Florida, 2018.

City of Palatka. "Bronson-Mulholland House." Accessed November 23, 2021. https://www.palatka-fl.gov/239/Bronson-Mulholland-House.

City of Tallahassee. "Old City Cemetery." Accessed January 13, 2022. https://www.talgov.com/realestate/res-coc-oldcity.aspx.

Codieck, Barrett. "Keepers of History, Shapers of Memory: The Florida Division of the United Daughters of the Confederacy, 1895–1930." Master's thesis, Florida State University, 2012.

Coles, David James. "Far from Fields of Glory: Military Operations in Florida during the Civil War 1864–1865." PhD diss., Florida State University, 1996.

Daytona Beach (FL) Observer.

Florida Master Site File. "Grand Army of the Republic Memorial Hall." Site file OS01258.

Florida Memory. "Old Confederate Soldiers and Sailors Home." Accessed November 23, 2021. https://www.floridamemory.com/discover/historical_records/confedhome/.

Glenwood Cemetery. "Notables." Accessed October 28, 2021. https://www.theglenwoodcemetery.com/notables/.

Grange, Roger T., Jr., and Dorothy L. Moore. *Smyrnea Settlement: Archaeology & History of an 18th Century British Plantation in East Florida.* New Smyrna Beach, FL: New Smyrna Museum of History, 2016. https://www.nsbhistory.org/smyrnea-settlement/.

Halifax Historical Society. *The Civil War in Volusia County: A Symposium April 24–26, 1987.* Daytona Beach, FL: Halifax Historical Society, 1987.

Hardy, Michael. "Biographies on Florida's Confederate Generals." *Looking for the Confederate War* (blog), December 9, 2020. http://michaelchardy.blogspot.com/2020/12/biographies-on-floridas-confederate.html.

———. "Site Visit Saturday: The Grave of Lewis Powell, alias Paine, Geneva, Florida." *Looking for the Confederate War* (blog), January 2, 2021. http://michaelchardy.blogspot.com/2021/01/site-visit-saturday-grave-of-lewis.html.

Hebel, Ianthe Bond. *Captain Simmons Bennett: An Early Pioneer and the Halifax River.* Five-page undated typescript.

Mandarin Museum. "Maple Leaf." Mandarin Museum and Historical Society. Accessed November 22, 2021. https://www.mandarinmuseum.net/mandarin-history/maple-leaf.

Mount Hebron Cemetery. "Stonewall Confederate Cemetery." Accessed January 25, 2022. https://www.mthebroncemetery.org/confederate-cemetery.html.

National Park Service. "National Register of Historic Places Inventory Form: Fort Jefferson National Monument." Accessed November 10, 2021. https://catalog.archives.gov/id/77843330.

———. "Dry Tortugas National Park, Florida." Last updated June 30, 2021. https://www.nps.gov/drto/index.htm.

———. "Native American Graves Protection and Repatriation Act." Last updated November 22, 2019. https://www.nps.gov/subjects/nagpra/index.htm.

Orlando (FL) Sentinel.

Ponce Inlet Lighthouse and Museum. "Lighthouse Keepers." Accessed December 9, 2021. https://www.ponceinlet.org/Lighthouse-Keepers-6-95.html.

St. Augustine (FL) Examiner.

St. Luke's Episcopal Church. "The St. Luke's Bible: A Legend about the Battle of Marianna, Florida." Accessed December 15, 2021. https://www.stlukesmarianna.org/content.cfm?id=314.

St. Paul's Rock Creek Cemetery. "Notable Burials." Accessed October 28, 2021. https://rockcreekcemetery.org/notable-burials/.

Sikes, Jo Anne, and Sandy Sammons. *Two Early Doctors.* Edgewater, FL: n.p., n.d.

Surratt Courier. Clinton, MD: Surratt Society.

Taylor, Dave. "The National Museum of Health and Medicine and the Lincoln Assassination." *Lincoln Conspirators.* June 1, 2014. https://lincolnconspirators.com/2014/06/01/the-national-museum-of-health-and-medicine-and-the-lincoln-assassination/.

Primary Sources

Doster, William E. "William E. Doster's Defense of Lewis Powell." *Famous Trials by Professor Douglas O. Linder.* University of Missouri Kansas City School of Law. Accessed October 27, 2021. https://famous-trials.com/lincoln/2177-defenseofpowell.

Fold3. Compiled Service Records of Confederate Soldiers Who Served in Organizations from the State of Florida. www.fold3.com.

Library of Congress. "Esther Hill Hawks Papers." Accessed January 12, 2022 https://www.loc.gov/item/mm79025304/.

National Archives and Records Administration. Case Files of Applications from Former Confederates for Presidential Pardons ("Amnesty Papers") 1865–1867. National Archives Microfilm Publication M1003, 73 rolls. Records of the Adjutant General's Office, 1780s–1917, Record Group 94. Washington, D.C.

———. 1860 U.S. census, population schedule. NARA microfilm publication M653, 1,438 rolls. Washington, D.C. Available through Ancestry.com.

———. Pardons under Amnesty Proclamations, compiled 1865–1869. A1 1005, 26 rolls. ARC ID: 638273. General Records of the Department of State, 1763–2002, Record Group 59. Washington, D.C.

United States Census Office and General Land Office. "U.S. Census for Central Florida, 1860." RICHES of Central Florida. Accessed December 29, 2021. https://richesmi.cah.ucf.edu/omeka/items/show/3832.

United States War Department. *Official Records of the Union and Confederate Navies.* 31 vols. Washington, D.C.: United States Government Printing Office, 1894–1922.

———. *The War of the Rebellion: A Compilation of the Official Records of the Union and Confederate Armies.* 128 vols., 3 series. Washington, D.C.: United States Government Printing Office, 1889.